ENJOY!

food you'll love

ENJOY!

food you'll love

Sheila Kiely

MERCIER PRESS

IRISH PUBLISHER – IRISH STORY

Take the time to cook and eat exactly what you want.

Just for you.

Sheila xx

Contents

Bread and Breakfast

Simple Suppers

Light and Veggie Dishes

Chicken and Duck Dishes

Dips

Relishes and Chutneys

Desserts and Sweets

Introduction

Cook what you want. Eat what you want. Eat for you.

AS A MOTHER OF SIX TEENAGERS, you can imagine that most of my cooking is aimed at satisfying them. If you've ever had to feed a teenager, you'll know that they are always starving and dinner is never ready soon enough. In my house the teens rarely pass through the kitchen without swinging out of the fridge.

Busy lives mean cooking is usually hurried and days don't revolve around meals, but rather are punctuated by them. My first book, *Gimme the Recipe*, was very much written to meet the needs of the everyday busy cook whose time is limited. But as time moves on and my children grow up and do more for themselves, I'm beginning to cook more for pleasure and for myself. I love food. I love reading about it and watching programmes on it, and it fascinates me that I have yet to taste all of the foods in the world. There is so much variety, there are so many cooking techniques and methods and there is always a new ingredient to discover.

The recipes in this book will still please the teenagers in my life now that they are more adventurous and grown-up, but this book is full of the food that I want to eat. *Gimme the Recipe* was everyday, delicious food, but it was about pleasing other people. This book is all about pleasing myself, and hopefully it will please you too.

Sheila

Acknowledgements

Creating a cookbook requires a lot of time and I am so grateful to my husband Denis for the blind eye he turned and the support he gave me as my desk groaned under the mounting pile of paperwork while I juggled our business with cookbook work. There was no shortage of honest feedback from our six children (Johnnie, Ellie, Daire, Eimear, Niall and Denny), who at one stage endured four nights in a row of pineapple upside-down cake until I got it exactly right. Children tell you the truth, so thank you!

When you hand over a cookbook script for editing you know there is no room for error and the editing process has to be fastidious. From the scrutiny of Wendy Logue the text transferred to Kristen Jensen, whose attention to detail is beyond scrupulous, and both of them have made this a better book. The final few glitches were picked up by Robert Doran, so thanks to all of you.

Working with food stylist Jette Virdi, photographer Marta Miklinska and graphic designer Sarah O'Flaherty during the photo shoot for the book was an incredible experience. Each brought great talent to the project and between them a balance and harmony emerged ensuring that each shot benefited from their collective creativity, flair and technical know-how, resulting in outstanding images.

To the 'Woodberry' girls and the book club gang, I know you will be kind in your reviews and thank you for your beautiful friendships, laughter and hugs.

Abina, thank you for your amazing baking, the hand-delivered warm Enniskeane breads and your wonderful company.

To Deirdre, my long-time running buddy and friend, thank you for the miles and milestones we've shared over the years and for the ones yet to come.

To my family, friends and in-laws, thank you for sharing so many celebrations around our table and for your love.

Finally a word of thanks to the team at Mercier Press, especially Mary Feehan, for their support and hard work behind the scenes to finish and now promote this book.

Store Cupboard
Essentials

The following long-life items are some of my favourites and are handy to have on standby.

Jams and Sauces

Cranberry sauce • Lemon curd • Apricot jam • Orange marmalade • Golden syrup
Runny honey • Wholegrain mustard • Mayonnaise • Chutney • Soy sauce
Sweet chilli sauce

Oils and Vinegars

Rapeseed oil • Coconut oil • Extra virgin olive oil • Extra virgin rapeseed oil
Toasted sesame oil • White wine vinegar • Red wine vinegar • Cider vinegar
Balsamic vinegar

Nuts and Seeds

Milled seeds (mixture) • Sesame seeds • Mixed whole nuts and seeds
Macadamia nuts • Cashew nuts

Herbs and Spices

Moroccan spice blend • Herbes de Provence • Sweet pimentón (dulce)
Smoked paprika • Paprika • Hot and mild chilli powder • Chilli flakes
Ras el hanout • Nutmeg • Garlic flakes • Turmeric • Ground cumin • Ground coriander
Ground cinnamon • Cardamom pods • Curry powder

Sugars

Dark muscovado sugar • Light brown sugar

Purées, Pestos and Pastes, etc.

Tomato purée • Harissa paste • Ginger purée • Red chilli paste • Garlic purée
Semi-sun-dried tomato pesto • Classic basil pesto • Sun-dried tomatoes

Chocolate and Dried Fruit

Dark chocolate (70%+) • Chocolate chips • Dried cranberries • Raisins
Desiccated coconut • Dried apricots

Canned Foods

Chopped tomatoes • Cannellini beans • Green lentils • Kidney beans • Chickpeas
Cooked artichoke hearts

Flours and Oats

Extra coarse wholewheat flour (I use Macroom Stoneground)
Porridge oats (I use Flahavan's 100% Wholegrain Organic)
Cornflour

In the Freezer

Garden peas • Chunks of fresh ginger • Puff pastry sheets
Pita breads • Flour tortillas

Stock Cubes

Beef, chicken and vegetable stock cubes

Booze

Brandy • Crème de cassis or kirsch

Oven *Heat* and *Temperatures*

Most electric ovens are multipurpose and will have a fan-assisted setting. I use the fan-assisted setting because it distributes the heat around the oven for more even, faster cooking than a conventional oven. If you use a conventional oven, you will need to increase the temperature given in these recipes by approximately 20–25°C and the cooking time will be a little longer too. (You should consult your cooker manual, as ovens vary.)

Note: Fan ovens are also known as convection ovens (as opposed to traditional conventional ovens).

Temperatures

All oven temperatures given in this book are in Celsius and are for fan-assisted ovens. The equivalent gas mark and Fahrenheit temperatures are given below.

Temperature Conversion Table

Fan oven	Conventional oven	Gas mark	Fahrenheit
90°C (very cool)	110°C	¼	225°F
110°C	130°C	½	265°F
120°C (cool)	140°C	1	285°F
130°C	150°C	2	300°F
140°C (moderate)	160°C	3	320°F
150°C	170°C	3	340°F
160°C	180°C	4	355°F
170°C (moderate hot)	190°C	5	375°F
180°C	200°C	6	390°F
190°C	210°C	6	410°F
200°C (hot)	220°C	7	430°F
210°C	230°C	8	450°F
220°C (very hot)	240°C	9	465°F

Bread

and

Breakfast

Porridge enthusiasts will swear that their way of making it is the best, and as this is my way, it is of course the best way. I usually slide into porridge-making mode somewhere around October or November, and it will continue to comfort me throughout the harsh winter months, usually into April, when I switch over to granola. Considered by many to be peasant food, this is a breakfast for kings.

Cinnamon and Apple Honeyed Porridge

Serves 2

80g porridge oats

550ml water

1 cooking apple

Honey (runny is best for swirling)

Ground cinnamon, to dust

A little milk or cream (optional)

1   Put the oats and water in a saucepan, cover and leave to soak overnight if you can (this will lead to quicker cooking and smoother porridge). For easier measuring, I usually use 2½ cups water to 1 cup porridge oats to serve two.

2   Prepare your cooking apple by slicing a shallow groove around the middle of it all the way around, cutting just through the skin. Place the prepared apple in a bowl, cover it and place it in the microwave to cook for 3–4 minutes while you cook the porridge. You want the apple cooked until tender and pulpy so it will be easy to scoop out of its skin. The cooking time will depend on the strength of your microwave and the size of the apple, so check it and use your judgement.

3   Cook the porridge over a medium heat, stirring with a wooden spoon more or less continuously for 3–4 minutes until it reaches your desired consistency.

4   Divide the porridge between two bowls. Scoop spoonfuls of the cooked apple pulp out of its skin and place on top of the cooked porridge. Drizzle with a little honey and sprinkle with a dusting of cinnamon. I like to add a little splash of milk too and then indulge. If it's your birthday, you really ought to add some cream.

I know that summer has finally arrived when my breakfast of choice becomes a bowl of ripe fresh fruit topped with a few tablespoons of yoghurt. A recent addition is a fortifying sprinkling of Linwoods' Milled Flax, Sunflower, Pumpkin and Sesame Seeds and Goji Berries, which is readily available in supermarkets and health-food stores. It's almost like having a fruity cheesecake for breakfast. Make up a large bowl of the fresh fruit doused in some lemon juice and it will keep well in the fridge for a couple of days.

Fruit and Yoghurt with Milled Seeds

Serves 1

Apple, cubed

Grapes, whole

Banana, sliced

Melon, cubed

Mandarin, segmented

Juice of ½ lemon

Greek yoghurt

Milled seeds of your choice

1   Assemble the prepared fruits in a large bowl and squeeze over the lemon juice. Serve topped with Greek yoghurt and generously sprinkled with milled seeds.

For a hurried summer's morning breakfast, granola with a dollop of natural yoghurt on top is the answer. It's even more satisfying if you've made the granola yourself, as it will be exactly to your liking and you won't have to pick out the raisins or the apricots or whatever it is that you're not particularly partial to.

As you watch TV of an evening, slip into the kitchen during the advertisements and assemble a tray with oats and whatever you fancy and leave it to toast awhile in the oven, then cool for the next morning's breakfast. The quantities given here would stretch to a week's worth of breakfasts, but that will depend on the number of portions and how indulgent they are.

Golden Granola

Makes 6 generous portions

150g porridge oats

150g combination of mixed dried fruit, nuts and seeds (you choose)

50g desiccated coconut (leave it out if you're not a fan)

4 tbsp golden syrup or runny honey

3 tbsp rapeseed oil

1   Preheat a fan oven to 160°C.

2   Mix the oats, mixed fruit, nuts and seeds and the desiccated coconut on a baking tray.

3   Drizzle the golden syrup or honey and the oil over them and mix thoroughly with a fork so that nothing is left completely dry.

4   Toast the granola mixture in the preheated oven for 25 minutes, tossing it with a fork at 5- or 10-minute intervals as it cooks to ensure even toasting. Leave to cool on the baking tray, then store in an airtight container.

5   To serve for breakfast, layer up the granola with some natural yoghurt and fruit.

For the days when you've got to grab something and run, wouldn't it be great to have a wholesome muffin on standby? These are given a kick of mixed spice, perfect for a mid-morning coffee.

Apple and Raisin Wholemeal Breakfast Muffins

Makes 12

350g extra coarse wholewheat flour

2 tsp baking powder

1 tsp mixed spice

150g light brown sugar, plus extra for sprinkling

Good handful of raisins

2 eggs, beaten

200ml natural yoghurt

4 tbsp sunflower oil

2 Pink Lady apples

1   Preheat a fan oven to 160°C. Line a 12-hole muffin tray with muffin cases.

2   Mix the flour, baking powder and mixed spice in a bowl, then add the brown sugar and the raisins.

3   Make a well in the centre and add the beaten eggs, natural yoghurt and sunflower oil. Mix together with a wooden spoon until just combined.

4   Peel and core the apples, then cut into small cubes and stir them through the muffin mixture.

5   Spoon the batter into the cases, crumble a little extra brown sugar on top of each one and bake in the oven for 35 minutes, until golden. Allow to cool on a wire rack.

Ah, soda bread, the bread of cheats. I love lazy baking, and as this soda bread doesn't require resting or kneading, it's super quick to make. I've been told by bakers that soda bread is the fast food of the bread world and that it's harder to digest because it doesn't prove, but as my mantra is a little of what you fancy does you good, I won't be saying no to soda bread any time soon. Given the addition of caramelised red onions, all the bread needs is a generous topping of your favourite cheese for a delicious lunch.

Caramelised Red Onion Soda Bread

Makes 1 loaf

400g plain flour, plus extra for dusting and shaping

1 tsp bicarbonate of soda

325ml buttermilk

4 tbsp caramelised red onion relish (page 150)

1 egg beaten with a splash of milk for the egg wash

1   Preheat a fan oven to 200°C. Place a baking tray in the oven to heat up.

2   Sift the flour and bicarbonate of soda into a bowl. Mix well with a fork to distribute the bicarbonate of soda evenly.

3   Make a well in the centre and pour in the buttermilk, then add the caramelised red onion relish. Mix together with a wooden spoon to form a gloopy dough, making sure the onions are well distributed.

4   Lightly dust the worktop with some flour and pour out the dough. Sprinkle a dusting of flour on the dough and on your hands, then shape the bread into a round. It will be sticky, so don't attempt to knead it.

5   Remove the heated baking tray from the oven and dust it with a little flour. Place the dough on the tray and score a cross on the top with a knife. Brush the top and sides with the egg wash.

6   Bake in the hot oven for 20 minutes, then reduce the heat to 170°C and bake for a further 10 minutes. The base of the bread should sound hollow when tapped. Allow to cool on a rack before slicing, though it's lovely served while still warm with a good thick layer of creamy cheese.

Simple
Suppers

Light and Veggie
Dishes

When you aren't in the mood for something heavy or overly filling but you still want something that will warm and cosset you from within, a soup like this can be just what you're after. I don't use fennel very often, but I love how special it makes this soup.

Carrot and Fennel Soup

Serves 4

1 fennel bulb

1 tbsp butter

8 medium carrots

750ml vegetable stock

Crusty bread, to serve

1 Cut the stalks and woody end off the fennel bulb and discard them, but reserve some of the delicate little fern-like fronds as a garnish. Finely dice the fennel.

2 Melt the butter in a saucepan over a low to medium heat. Add the diced fennel, cover the pan and allow to sweat for a few minutes, until softened.

3 Meanwhile, peel and chop the carrots. Add them to the softened fennel, then add the vegetable stock. Bring to the boil, then reduce to a simmer for 20–30 minutes, until the carrots are tender. Blend the soup until smooth (handheld stick blenders are excellent for this job). Ladle into bowls and garnish with the reserved fennel fronds. Delicious served with crusty bread.

We all have days when we can't be bothered to cook, but you still have to eat, so it should be something balanced and tasty. The ultimate cheese and ham toastie is a complete meal and a simple, satisfying supper. One of my favourite condiments to have on standby is a jar of cranberry sauce, and a good smearing of this takes a basic ham and cheese to your plate in style.

Cranberry Croque Monsieur

Serves 1

2 slices of granary or multigrain wholewheat bread

Butter

Cranberry sauce

Cooked ham slices

Cheddar cheese slices

Rocket leaves

Red onion, thinly sliced

1 Heat the sandwich toaster or grill. Butter both sides of the bread, then smear one side with a generous layer of cranberry sauce. Cover with slices of ham and cheese and a scattering of rocket leaves and sliced onion. Close the sandwich and toast or grill until golden brown and enjoy.

You may be tired after a long day and want something filling to eat, but not another stodgy pizza that's going to make you feel like a beached whale later and have you trying to 'be good' tomorrow. It needs to be quick too. So how quick is this? It takes about 20 minutes total to cook, so I'd say that's fairly quick. And it's not only delicious and nutritious, but it's also incredibly tasty and filling. The ciabatta croutons are an optional extra that will add crunch, but leave them out if you want to err on the side of being super healthy.

Roast Squash and Legume Soup with Ciabatta Croutons

Serves 4–6

For the soup

1 butternut squash

2 tbsp rapeseed oil

2 onions

2 garlic cloves

1 x 400g tin of whole peeled plum tomatoes

1 x 400g tin of chickpeas

1 x 400g tin of kidney beans

500ml vegetable stock (low-salt and organic if possible)

2 tsp herbes de Provence

Good handful of fresh flat-leaf parsley

For the ciabatta croutons

Day-old ciabatta

1–2 tbsp rapeseed oil

1 Preheat a fan oven to 180°C.

2 To make the croutons, cut the ciabatta into bite-size chunks. Heat the oil in a frying pan over a medium to high heat and lightly brown the croutons on both sides. Drain the croutons on a plate lined with kitchen paper to absorb any excess oil.

3 Peel and deseed the butternut squash and cut into chunks. Place on a baking tray and drizzle with 1 tablespoon of the oil. Roast in the hot oven for 15–20 minutes, until tender.

4 Meanwhile, peel and chop the onions into smallish chunks. Heat the remaining tablespoon of oil over a low heat in a medium or large saucepan, then add the onions and leave to soften for 5 minutes. Peel and crush the garlic cloves, then add to the onions to cook for a further 2 minutes.

5 Whizz the plum tomatoes in a mini-chopper or food processor or break them up with a fork before adding to the softening onion and garlic.

6 Drain and rinse the chickpeas and kidney beans and add to the saucepan along with the vegetable stock and herbes de Provence. Bring to the boil, then reduce to a simmer for 10–15 minutes.

7 Finely chop the parsley and stir most of it in. Add the chunks of roasted butternut squash, then ladle into bowls and garnish with ciabatta croutons and the rest of the finely chopped parsley to serve.

As the name suggests, this soup is for the depths of winter, when the cold is seeping into your bones or perhaps when the heating is yet again out of action and you really need warming up. This is one for the black pepper lovers – it will leave your mouth and lips gently tingling.

Winter Warmer Peppered Parsnip, Potato and Leek Soup

Serves 4

2 small or 1 large leek

50g butter

2 medium parsnips (approx. 450g)

2 medium (approx. 450g) floury potatoes, e.g. Rooster

2 tsp ground black pepper

1 tsp salt

1 litre vegetable stock

Fresh flat-leaf parsley, to garnish

1   Top and tail the leeks, removing the outer layer of leaves if they are very coarse or dirty. Rinse under running cold water, then slice in half lengthways and thinly slice again into half-moons.

2   Melt the butter in a large saucepan over a low heat. Add the sliced leeks and cover with a lid to sweat for 10 minutes.

3   Peel and cube the parsnips and potatoes, then add to the softened leeks with the ground black pepper and salt, mixing well. Add the vegetable stock and bring to the boil, then reduce the heat to a simmer, with the lid almost covering the pan, for 30 minutes. Blend well with a stick blender or in a food processor. Serve with some finely chopped fresh parsley.

It's been said that detoxing is nonsense and that your kidneys and liver take care of all that. However, after a particularly indulgent season, such as the Christmas holiday period, it will do you good to take a break from fatty overloading and to eat lighter foods for a day or two. To make this a detox soup meant cutting out the fat from the butter, the starch from the potato and the salt from the stock that I would normally add to a soup. Instead, I use a little organic coconut oil to soften the onions and a good dose of ground cumin for flavour. The fresh parsley adds flavour too, and it might surprise you to learn that it's also a good source of iron. This is a great soup to have on standby in the fridge when you're starving and trying to be good.

Feel Good Vegetable Soup

Serves 4

1 medium onion

1 tsp coconut oil

3 large carrots

1 parsnip

1 small swede or turnip

2 tsp ground cumin

1 litre low-salt vegetable stock

2 tbsp chopped fresh flat-leaf parsley

Freshly ground black pepper

1 Peel and finely chop the onion. Heat the coconut oil in a saucepan over a low heat. Add the chopped onion and leave to soften with the lid on for 10 minutes.

2 Meanwhile, peel and dice the carrots, parsnip and the swede or turnip and set aside.

3 Raise the heat to medium, then add the cumin to the softened onion and stir well. Cook for 1 minute, then add the diced vegetables and mix well. Add the stock and bring to the boil, then reduce the heat to a simmer for 20 minutes.

4 Rinse and finely chop the parsley and add most of it to the soup before liquidising it. Use the remaining parsley to garnish the soup and season with some black pepper.

Delicious. Not too many ingredients and even more flavoursome on day 2. Perfect to make for dinner on a Monday, bring to work for lunch on a Tuesday and freeze a portion for one of those Friday nights when you're too ravenous and tired to even wait for a takeaway delivery. Perfect 'you' food.

Cauliflower and Sweet Potato Curry

Serves 4

5 cardamom pods

1 medium onion

1 tbsp rapeseed or coconut oil

Thumb-sized chunk of fresh ginger

2 garlic cloves

1 tbsp garam masala

1 tsp mild chilli powder

1 tsp ground turmeric

1 large cauliflower (approx. 750g)

1 large sweet potato (approx. 500g)

200ml tomato passata

500ml vegetable stock

250ml water

Boiled rice, to serve (optional)

1 Bash the cardamom pods – a pestle and mortar is good for this job – to release the seeds, and discard the husks.

2 Finely chop the onion. Heat the oil in a large saucepan over a low heat and soften the onions for 5 minutes.

3 Grate the ginger and peel and crush the garlic, then add them to the softened onion and mix well. Turn the heat up to medium and add the cardamom seeds, garam masala, chilli powder and turmeric and cook for 1 minute.

4 Break the cauliflower into florets and cut the sweet potato into large bite-size chunks. Add these to the pan, mixing well to coat with the spices, then add the passata and mix well.

5 Pour in the vegetable stock and enough water to almost cover the vegetables.

6 Bring to the boil, then reduce the heat and simmer with the lid almost covering the pan for 40 minutes, until the vegetables are tender. Serve as is or with rice.

Note: Store ginger in the freezer and grate it as needed, frozen and unpeeled, with a Microplane grater.

Too often, vegetarian burgers are lightweight and unsatisfying. What I like about these is that they look meaty and are robust and filling. The patties can be prepared ahead of time and left in the fridge until you're ready to cook.

Spiced Vegetarian Burgers
Serves 6

3 slices of multigrain wholewheat bread (approx. 170g)

1 medium onion

2 tbsp rapeseed or coconut oil

100g mushrooms

2 garlic cloves

2 tsp regular paprika

1 tsp hot chilli powder

1 x 400g tin of lentils

1 x 400g tin of kidney beans

1 egg, beaten

Cornflour, for dusting

Baps, buns or bread rolls, to serve

1   Blitz the bread in a food processor or mini-chopper to create breadcrumbs and set aside.

2   Finely chop the onion and soften in 1 tablespoon of oil heated in a large frying pan over a low heat, for 5 minutes. Finely chop the mushrooms and peel and crush the garlic, then add them to the softened onion and cook for 3 minutes. Add the paprika and chilli powder and mix well.

3   Drain the lentils in a sieve and press to squeeze out any excess moisture, then stir them into the onion and mushrooms. Take the pan off the heat.

4   Roughly pulse the well-drained kidney beans in a food processor – you want them bitey, not pulpy. Put these in a large bowl, then mix in the breadcrumbs, the lentil mixture and the beaten egg to combine. Use your hands to shape into six even-sized patties. Lightly dust the tops of the burgers with cornflour.

5   Heat the remaining tablespoon of oil in large frying pan over a medium to high heat. Cook as many burgers as will fit in the pan for 5 minutes, floured side down. Lightly dust the other side with cornflour before turning the burgers over and cooking for a further 5 minutes.

6   Serve in lightly toasted buns or baps. I suggest serving them with coleslaw, lettuce and ketchup too.

The beauty of a tagine, like any stew, really, is that once the preparation is done, it's a quick assembly of all the ingredients and then it can be left to its own devices, giving you a bit of time to get on with living. If you don't have an actual tagine pot, just use a regular casserole pot. This is a hot, steaming plate of vegetable goodness that really hits the spot.

Vegetable Tagine

Serves 4

1 large onion

2 tbsp rapeseed or coconut oil

3 garlic cloves

2 tsp Moroccan spice blend

1 x 400g tin of chickpeas

125g raisins

450ml vegetable stock

2 tbsp tomato purée

350g carrots

350g sweet potatoes

2 tsp runny honey

Small bunch of fresh coriander, chopped

Seeds of 1 pomegranate (optional)

Lemon and coriander couscous (page 118) or pea and mint bulgur wheat salad (page 119), to serve

1   Preheat a fan oven to 160°C.

2   Roughly chop the onion. Heat the oil in a large pan over a medium heat. Add the onion and let it soften for 5 minutes. Peel and crush the garlic cloves, then add them to the pan and cook for 1 minute. Add the Moroccan spices and mix to coat everything. Cook for 1 minute more.

3   Drain and rinse the canned chickpeas and add to the pan along with the raisins, vegetable stock and tomato purée. Reduce the heat to low.

4   Peel and cut the carrots and sweet potatoes into even-sized chunks. Add the prepared vegetables to the pan along with the honey and most of the chopped coriander. Mix everything together well and transfer to a tagine or casserole dish.

5   Place the tagine or casserole dish into the oven for 2 hours, until all the vegetables are tender (a knife should easily slide through the veg). Serve with the remaining chopped coriander and the pomegranate seeds sprinkled on top, if using. This is really good served with couscous or a bulgur wheat salad.

I wouldn't hesitate to make a batch of this lasagne and eat it myself every day for a week. Just switch up the sides of salads or vegetables and you'll have all the variety you require. Cooking the lentils with a clove of garlic and then introducing mushrooms, more heady garlic, pungent oregano and the depth of tomato purée gives this all the flavour you'll need.

Vegetarian Lasagne

Makes 6 large portions

250g green speckled lentils or Puy lentils (see the note below)

4 garlic cloves

2 medium onions

3 tbsp rapeseed oil, plus a little extra

300g mushrooms

2 tsp oregano

1 x 400g tin of chopped tomatoes

3 tbsp tomato purée

3 tbsp water

250g ricotta cheese

75g grated Parmesan, plus a little extra

150ml crème fraîche (approx. 6 tbsp)

2 tbsp basil pesto

Fresh lasagne pasta sheets

1 Place the lentils in a saucepan and cover with cold water. Add a peeled clove of garlic and bring to the boil for 5 minutes. Reduce the heat and simmer for a further 15–20 minutes, then drain, removing and discarding the garlic clove.

2 Meanwhile, roughly chop the onions. Heat 2 tablespoons of the rapeseed oil in a large pan over a low heat, then add the onions and let them soften for 5 minutes. Peel and crush the three remaining garlic cloves. Add to the softened onion, stir through and cook for 1 minute.

3 Chop the mushrooms into bite-size pieces. Turn the heat up and add them to the pan of onions along with the oregano and another tablespoon of oil. Stir through and cook for a couple of minutes, until the mushrooms start to colour.

4 Add the tin of chopped tomatoes and the cooked, drained lentils. Stir well, then add the tomato purée and water. Reduce to a simmer for a couple of minutes while you prepare the cheesy sauce.

5 Preheat a fan oven to 180°C.

6 Mix the ricotta, grated Parmesan, crème fraîche and basil pesto together in a bowl to a thick sauce consistency. If you need to loosen it up a little, add some oil.

7 Layer up the lasagne in a large ovenproof baking dish – spread half of the lentil mix on the base of the dish and top with a layer of lasagne sheets, then the remaining lentil mix, half of the cheese sauce, a layer of lasagne sheets, then the remaining cheese sauce. Top with a little grated Parmesan and cook in the oven for 30 minutes, until the cheese is turning golden brown.

Note: Follow the directions on your packet of lentils for cooking – the ones I buy don't require pre-soaking, but some do. Feel free to substitute a drained tin of pre-cooked lentils if you prefer and leave out a clove of garlic as you will not need to cook them as per the first instruction.

This could be a side dish, but from time to time I like to go meatless and I love cheesy potatoes. This is an indulgent dish that I eat a large portion of with a simple baby leaf salad. If you have the misfortune of having to feed someone else too, someone who is perhaps muttering 'Where is the meat?', you could point them in the direction of the fridge and a packet of rashers.

Creamy Cheese and Onion Potato Bake

Serves 6 as a side or 4 as a main

8–10 medium floury potatoes, e.g. Roosters, skins on and scrubbed well

2 medium onions

Large knob of butter, plus extra for greasing

250ml milk

250ml single cream

75g grated Cheddar cheese

Small handful of fresh flat-leaf parsley

1   Preheat a fan oven to 180°C. Lightly grease a large baking dish with a little butter.

2   Thinly slice the scrubbed potatoes, leaving the skins on. Parboil the potato slices for 5 minutes or so, until they're starting to get tender.

3   Meanwhile, peel and thinly slice the onions. Melt the butter in a large saucepan over a low heat and soften the onions for 5 minutes.

4   Drain the potato slices and place half of them in the base of the greased baking dish. Place the softened onions on top and cover with the remaining potatoes. Pour over the milk and cream, then scatter the grated cheese on top and cover the baking dish with tinfoil.

5   Bake for 30 minutes, then remove the foil and bake for 10 minutes more, until the potatoes are tender and the top is golden. Garnish with a generous sprinkling of chopped fresh parsley.

Eight Ways with Baked Potatoes

What could be simpler than to place a large scrubbed potato into a hot oven (fan 200°C) for 45 minutes or so (depending on size) and then indulge with lashings of melted butter, salt and pepper? Eating the skin is a must, as it harbours so much goodness and fibre. Now that's a simple supper.

Here are eight different directions in which to take your baked potato: Mexican, Hungarian, French, Italian, American and Greek.

1   Heated kidney beans with chopped fresh red chilli, sprinkled with chopped fresh flat-leaf parsley and finished with a dollop of Greek yoghurt.

2   Spiced ratatouille – soften some chopped onions, garlic, peppers and celery in oil with a dash of smoked paprika.

3   Herby lentils – simply soften a chopped onion in a little oil with some herbes de Provence, then add a tin of drained lentils and heat through.

4   Brie, cranberry sauce and rocket leaves.

5   Crispy fried pancetta, grated Parmesan and rocket leaves.

6   Basil pesto and diced cooked chicken breast with halved cherry tomatoes.

7   Garlic butter and peppered sweetcorn kernels – heat a tin of sweetcorn, add a knob of garlic butter and season generously with salt and freshly ground black pepper.

8   Halved black olives, feta cubes, sliced beef tomato, sliced red onion and a drizzle of rapeseed oil.

Chicken and Duck
Dishes

Some years, if the notion takes me, I bake a proper traditional Christmas cake. When I do, I'm left with a jar of apricot jam of which only a little has been used to stick the marzipan to the cake. Here's a recipe where you can take that apricot jam from the back of the fridge and use it to make a tasty, sticky apricot chicken dish that I like to serve with the apricot couscous on page 117.

Sticky Apricot Chicken

Serves 4

1 tbsp rapeseed or coconut oil

4 skinless chicken breasts

1 medium onion

2 tbsp apricot jam

250ml chicken stock

Apricot couscous (page 117), to serve

1 Preheat a fan oven to 180°C.

2 Heat the oil in a large frying pan over a medium to high heat. Cook the chicken breasts for a couple of minutes on each side to brown them lightly, then transfer them to a baking tray and place in the oven to continue cooking.

3 Peel and thinly slice the onion and add it to the same frying pan that you used to cook the chicken, scraping up any browned bits and juices from the bottom of the pan. Leave the onion to soften over a low to medium heat for 5 minutes. Add the apricot jam to the softened onion and pour in the chicken stock, mixing well.

4 Bring to the boil, then reduce the heat to medium. Add the chicken breasts back into the pan from the oven. Simmer for about 10 minutes, turning the chicken occasionally as the sauce cooks and reduces a little. Test that the chicken is cooked by cutting through to the centre – there should be no trace of pink. Serve with the apricot couscous.

Quick and filling yet fresh and light, this is perfect summer dining. All it needs to accompany it is something chilled, crisp and white for the grown-ups to drink.

Using pre-cooked chicken fillets left over from the previous night's dinner makes this dish super speedy, but if you don't happen to have any leftover chicken, you could use some chopped cooked ham or crisp up some bacon instead. The first time I made this dish I used lettuce pesto, but regular basil pesto is perfect too.

Fusilli Summer Chicken

Serves 4

350g fusilli pasta

200g frozen garden peas

3 pre-cooked chicken breasts (or chopped cooked ham or cook up some rashers)

1 spring onion

5 tbsp lettuce pesto (page 143) or basil pesto, plus extra to serve

Grated Parmesan, to garnish

1   Boil a large saucepan of water and cook the pasta according to the instructions on the packet.

2   Boil a medium saucepan of water and put the peas on to cook.

3   Slice the cooked chicken and add it to the pasta about 1 minute from the end of its cooking time to heat it through. (If you're using cooked ham or cooked rashers, add them after the pasta has been drained.)

4   Drain the cooked pasta and chicken and the peas and toss them together in a serving bowl. Chop the spring onion and stir it in along with the pesto to lightly coat everything. Serve with grated Parmesan and extra pesto on the side.

What's not to love about a tray bake? This is one of those rare dishes that results in minimal washing up and cooks away by itself, allowing you to get on with things.

Mediterranean Chicken and Vegetables with Homemade Ketchup

Serves 4

4 chicken pieces (drumsticks, thighs, breast on bone etc.), skin on

4 large floury potatoes, e.g. Roosters, skin on and scrubbed well

Rapeseed oil

Sea salt and freshly ground black pepper

2 sweet red peppers

1–2 red onions

1 aubergine

6 garlic cloves

1 tsp herbes de Provence

For the homemade ketchup (makes 1 ramekin)

5 tbsp tomato purée

2 tbsp rapeseed oil

1½ tbsp balsamic vinegar

½ tsp garlic granules

1   Preheat a fan oven to 180°C.

2   Place the chicken pieces into a large roasting tin.

3   Slice the unpeeled potatoes into half-inch rounds and place in the tin around the chicken. (You may need to cook some on a separate tray if the roasting tin is too crowded.)

4   Drizzle a lillle rapeseed oil over thc chicken and potatoes and season generously with sea salt and freshly ground black pepper. Place the tin in the oven and cook for 20 minutes.

5   Meanwhile, deseed and slice the red peppers and peel the onion(s) and cut into eight pieces. Set aside.

6   Don't prepare the aubergine until the chicken has been cooking for 20 minutes; otherwise it will discolour. Rinse and slice the aubergine into half-inch rounds, then cut each round into four pieces. Remove the roasting tray from the oven and add the peppers, red onion and aubergine chunks around the chicken.

7   You can leave the skin on the garlic cloves and lightly squash them with the side of a knife, then poke these in around the chicken as well. Drizzle some more oil on the vegetables and sprinkle with the herbes de Provence.

8   Raise the oven temperature to 200°C and cook for a further 20 minutes, until the chicken is cooked through.

9   While that's cooking, mix the tomato purée with the rapeseed oil, balsamic vinegar and garlic granules. Adjust the quantities of vinegar and garlic granules to your taste.

10   Serve the chicken with a drizzle of homemade ketchup over the top.

Pimentón (Spanish paprika) varies in strength, from sweet (*dulce*) to medium (*agridulce*) to hot (*picante*) and it also comes in smoked varieties (*de la Vera*). It's made from sweet and hot dried peppers. I remember watching Rick Stein's *Spain* programme on TV and being fascinated to see that the ingredients of chorizo are simply pork meat and Spanish pimentón.

Pimentón Chicken with Spicy Sweet Potato and Carrot Mash

Serves 4

Rapeseed oil

4 skinless chicken breasts

1 tsp sweet pimentón (*dulce*)

Spicy sweet potato and carrot mash (page 114), to serve

1 Heat a heavy-based, non-stick frying pan over a medium to high heat. Drizzle some oil onto a plate and dip the chicken breasts in it to coat them. Sear the outside of the chicken breasts for a minute on both sides, then turn down the heat.

2 Use a sharp knife to cut along and through the side of each chicken breast and splay it wide open. Cooking them like this – butterflied – will ensure they cook quickly right through to the centre.

3 Sprinkle the chicken with the pimentón and cook both sides of the chicken for a couple of minutes each. Then sprinkle with pimentón again before you turn it over and continue to cook until cooked through. Delicious served on a bed of spicy sweet potato and carrot mash.

Here's a tasty, quick and easy dish for the weekend. I use the ras el hanout as a simple rub on the chicken and then pan-fry it in strips. The accompanying spicy chickpea mash has a nice bit of chilli heat and you're getting some lustre and shine into your skin from the avocados.

Ras el Hanout Spiced Chicken with Chickpea Mash and Avocado Mash

Serves 4

3–4 skinless chicken fillets

1 tbsp ras el hanout

2 tbsp rapeseed or coconut oil

1 x 400g tin of chickpeas

2 small handfuls of fresh coriander

1 fresh red chilli

2 garlic cloves

1 tsp ground cumin

2 ripe avocados

Sea salt and freshly ground black pepper

1 lime, to serve

1   Cut each chicken fillet into five or six long strips and place them in a bowl. Sprinkle over the ras el hanout and use your hands to evenly coat the chicken with the spice blend.

2   Heat 1 tablespoon of the oil in a large frying pan over a medium to high heat and fry the chicken strips for 5–8 minutes, until cooked through.

3   Drain and rinse the chickpeas, then blitz them with half of the fresh coriander in a food processor. Chop the remaining coriander and set it aside.

4   Deseed and finely chop the red chilli. Peel and crush the garlic. Heat the remaining tablespoon of oil in a medium-sized saucepan over a medium heat. Add the chilli and garlic and cook for 1 minute. Add the cumin and cook for 1 minute more, then stir in the blitzed chickpeas to heat through.

5   Slice the avocados in half, remove the stones and scoop the flesh into a bowl. Mash this with the chopped coriander and season with salt and pepper.

6   Serve the chicken strips with the chickpea mash and avocado mash, with lime wedges on the side.

I have to admit that I was very surprised when this experimental dish got the thumbs up in my house. Complaints were anticipated from the 'It's too spicy' and the 'Where's the gravy?' brigades, but none were forthcoming. Because it's served in bowls and eaten with a fork, this dish has the bonus of creating minimal washing up. It's a true one-pot dish with no accompaniments required. And with plenty of vegetables and minimum fat, it's healthy to boot.

Jambalaya Chicken

Serves 6

1 tbsp rapeseed or coconut oil

4 skinless chicken breasts

3cm chunk of fresh ginger

4 garlic cloves

2 tbsp ras el hanout

1 large red onion

1 tbsp dark brown sugar

2 red peppers

2 fresh green chillies

2 x 400g tins of chopped tomatoes

500ml hot chicken stock

350g basmati rice

Coriander to garnish (optional)

1   In a large, hob-proof casserole dish or pan, heat the oil over a medium heat. Add the chicken breasts and cook for 2 minutes on each side, then cut the semi-cooked chicken into chunks in the pan. Grate the ginger and peel and crush the garlic cloves, then add them to the pan and cook for 1 minute. Add the ras el hanout, mix well and cook for 1 minute.

2   Cut the red onion into large wedges and add them to the pan along with the brown sugar.

3   Mix everything together and cook for 1 minute.

4   Deseed and slice the red peppers and deseed and finely chop the green chillies, then add them to the pan. Stir in the chopped tomatoes and bring to the boil, then reduce to a simmer for 10 minutes.

5   Pour in the hot chicken stock and scatter the basmati rice on top, pressing it down into the liquid. Bring to the boil, then cover the dish or pan and reduce to a simmer for a further 10 minutes, until the rice is cooked. You may want to add a little more water as the rice cooks if you feel it's getting too dried out.

6   Serve with a garnish of coriander if you like.

This is one of those simple dishes where very little preparation is required and it works its magic in the oven. Pastry can be quite heavy and calorific, so it's best to serve this with a virtuous side of salad. I line the pastry with cranberry sauce and fill the chicken with some softened red onion, herbs, cheese and cooked ham, but it would also work well filled with some chopped mushrooms or simply some garlic butter.

Herbed Cranberry Chicken in Puff Pastry with Brie and Ham

Serves 4

1 medium red onion

1 tbsp coconut or rapeseed oil

Small handful of fresh flat-leaf parsley or 1 tsp dried parsley

A few fresh thyme sprigs or 1 tsp dried thyme

1 large or 2 medium ready-made puff pastry sheet(s), thawed

2–3 tbsp cranberry sauce (optional)

4 skinless chicken breasts

4 slices of Brie

4 thick slices of cooked ham (optional)

1 egg, beaten

Green salad, to serve

1   Preheat a fan oven to 200°C. Place a baking tray in the oven to heat it up.

2   Peel and finely chop the red onion. Heat the oil in a small frying pan over a medium heat and soften the onion for 5 minutes. Finely chop the fresh parsley and the thyme leaves. Take the frying pan off the heat and stir in the herbs, whether fresh or dried.

3   Open up the pastry sheet(s) and use a knife to generously smear with cranberry sauce (if using).

4   Divide the pastry into four triangles (one for each chicken breast). Set a chicken breast in the centre of each triangle and carefully slice open the side of each chicken breast about halfway through to create a pocket. Stuff each chicken breast with a slice of Brie, a slice of ham (if using) and a few teaspoons of the softened red onion and herbs. Carefully wrap the pastry around the chicken like a blanket, folding up the bottom of the pastry first and then bringing in the two sides, leaving one end of the chicken exposed.

5   Place the wrapped chicken on the heated baking tray. Brush with the beaten egg and cook for 30 minutes, until puffed up and golden. Serve with a simple salad.

Recipes for slow cookers can be so disappointing because so many of them expect you to sear the meat before cooking, which to me defeats the purpose of having a slow cooker! I want to pop the ingredients into it and leave it to work away for several hours with the minimal amount of input or effort. There is only 5 or 10 minutes of preparation for this dish.

Honey and Ginger Slow Cooker Chicken

Serves 4

4 skinless chicken breasts

1 medium white onion

1 red pepper

4–5 tbsp low-salt soy sauce

3 tbsp white wine vinegar

2 tbsp honey

1 tbsp ginger purée (or small chunk of fresh ginger, grated)

2 tsp garlic purée (or 1–2 garlic cloves, crushed)

1 tsp red chilli paste (or ½–1 fresh red chilli, finely diced)

Boiled rice, to serve

2 spring onions, chopped, to garnish

1 Place the chicken in the base of the slow cooker. Peel and chop the onion into chunks and deseed and chop the red pepper into strips, then scatter them on top of the chicken.

2 Mix the soy sauce, vinegar, honey, ginger purée, garlic purée and red chilli paste in a small jug or cup and pour it over the chicken and vegetables. Place the lid on top and cook for 4 hours on high or 6–8 hours on low. Ensure that the chicken is piping hot in the middle and not at all pink.

3 Serve over boiled rice and garnish with chopped spring onions.

What is your favourite sandwich? For many Irish people the traditional sandwich of choice is chicken and stuffing. If I can resist any leftovers from this dish, they'll definitely go into a chicken and stuffing sandwich the next day. This dish is made Christmassy with cranberry sauce and there are enough carbs in the stuffing to make this more than filling, but if absolutely necessary you could accompany it with a side of the paprika roast baby potatoes on page 130.

Parsley and Thyme Stuffed Chicken with Red Cabbage

Serves 4

1 large or 2 small onions

50g butter

3 slices of wholewheat bread (see note)

2 tsp dried parsley

2 tsp dried thyme

½ tsp salt

4 skinless chicken breasts

4 cocktail sticks, for assembly

2 tbsp cranberry sauce

2 tbsp rapeseed oil

For the red cabbage

½ head of red cabbage

1 tbsp rapeseed oil

2 tbsp red wine vinegar

Fresh nutmeg

1 tbsp runny honey

1   Preheat a fan oven to 180°C. Get a small baking tray ready for the chicken breasts – you want to cook them close together to retain their juices, so a tray that's only just big enough is best.

2   Peel and finely chop the onion (a mini-chopper works best for this). Melt the butter in a large saucepan over a low heat. Add the chopped onion, cover the pan and leave to sweat for 10 minutes.

3   Blitz the bread in a food processor or mini-chopper to create breadcrumbs. Once the onions are cooked, take the saucepan off the heat and add the breadcrumbs, herbs and salt, stirring well to combine.

4   Slit the side of each chicken breast to create a pocket. Take a fistful of stuffing and squeeze it to compact it, then stuff the breast with it, securing the side with a cocktail stick. Shape any leftover stuffing into compact round stuffing dumplings to cook alongside the chicken.

5   Mix the cranberry sauce and rapeseed oil together really well in a small bowl. Use a pastry brush to thickly paint the chicken breasts with the sauce – use it all up.

6   Cook the chicken in the preheated oven for 20 minutes, then turn up the heat to 200°C for another 5 minutes. Check that the chicken is fully cooked through – there should be no traces of pink.

7   While the chicken cooks, prepare the cabbage. Use a food processor to grate the cabbage. Heat the oil in a large saucepan over a low heat. Add the grated cabbage, cover the pan and sweat for 10 minutes. Raise the heat and pour in the red wine vinegar and a good grating of fresh nutmeg. Stir well for 2 minutes. Reduce the heat to low and cook, covered, for a further 10 minutes, then stir through the honey to heat it.

8   Divide the red cabbage between four shallow bowls or plates and serve with the chicken on top.

Note: I like to use a multi-seed wholemeal bread for extra texture when making breadcrumbs.

Sweetened with orange juice, this is quick and easy to prepare and ready in 20 minutes. I love it with brown rice or noodles.

Sweet and Sticky Chicken Stir-Fry

Serves 4

4 skinless chicken breasts

1 tbsp coconut or rapeseed oil

½ head of broccoli

200g mangetout

3 spring onions

3 tbsp dark soy sauce

Juice of 2 oranges

2 tsp cornflour

Handful of cashew nuts

Cooked brown rice or noodles, to serve

1 Chop the chicken into bite-size pieces. Heat the oil in a wok or large frying pan and cook the chicken for 4 minutes on a high heat.

2 While the chicken is cooking, break the broccoli into small florets, rinse the mangetout and rinse and chop the spring onions.

3 Add 1 tablespoon of the soy sauce to the chicken, then add the broccoli, mangetout and spring onions and cook for 3 minutes.

4 Juice the oranges and mix with the cornflour and the remaining 2 tablespoons of soy sauce in a small bowl. Add this to the chicken and cook for 1 minute, stirring well. If you would prefer a saucier mix, add a little water. Finally, sprinkle in the cashew nuts and cook for 1 minute. Serve with rice or noodles.

These simple, quick burgers are great for speedy summer eating. I like to use multigrain ciabattas instead of standard burger buns. Adjust the quantities as required.

Simple Spiced Chicken Burgers

Serves 1

1 chicken fillet

Ground cumin

Curry powder

Freshly ground black pepper

Plain flour

Coconut or rapeseed oil, for frying

Multi-seed ciabatta or burger bun

Coleslaw, rocket leaves and thinly sliced red onion, to serve

1   Use a rolling pin to bash and flatten the chicken fillet for quicker cooking.

2   Assemble a spice plate by mixing together some ground cumin, curry powder, freshly ground black pepper and a little flour, then dip the flattened chicken fillet in this, making sure it's coated on both sides.

3   Heat some oil in a large frying pan or griddle pan. Cook the coated chicken fillet on each side for a few minutes, until nicely coloured and cooked through.

4   Cut the fillet to size to fill your ciabatta or burger bun and load it up with some coleslaw, rocket leaves and sliced red onion.

Note: Use one chicken fillet per person, so just multiply up if you are making this for more than one.

We've a lot of noodle bars and restaurants popping up in our locality, and while my kids adore Pad Thai, I'll always go for the curry and rice instead. Recently I had a delicious red massaman curry and I couldn't believe the amount of vegetables it contained. This is my version. It will make a big pot of curry and is a good one for a nice relaxed evening of entertaining, as you can prepare it ahead of time. It's a real crowd-pleaser.

Red Massaman Chicken

Serves 8

Note on equipment

As this makes a large quantity, you need to have:

- 1 large, wide frying pan to cook the chicken with the massaman paste

- 1 large frying pan or griddle pan to cook the vegetables separately

- 1 large saucepan to combine the chicken and vegetables

- Mini-chopper and/or food processor with a fine julienne attachment or a julienne peeler for the carrots

350g baby potatoes (approx. 8–10) • 1 medium onion • 2 tbsp rapeseed or coconut oil
4 chicken breasts • ½ red pepper • 4 spring onions • 150g fine green beans
150g mangetout • 1 carrot, peeled and julienned • 250g cherry tomatoes
750ml vegetable stock • 1 x 400ml tin of full-fat coconut milk
Handful of salted peanuts, roughly crushed, to serve

For the massaman paste

5 cardamom pods • ½ red pepper, deseeded and roughly chopped
2 garlic cloves, peeled • Thumb-size chunk of fresh ginger, grated
2 tbsp lemongrass paste (or 2 lemongrass stalks, finely chopped)
2 tbsp fish sauce • 2 tsp hot chill powder • 1 tsp ground coriander
1 tsp ground cumin • 1 tsp ground turmeric

1   Microwave the baby potatoes, skin on, with a splash
    of water for about 4 minutes, until firm but just turning
    tender. Cut in half and set aside.

2   Finely chop the onion. Heat 1 tablespoon of the oil in a
    large, wide frying pan over a low heat. Add the chopped
    onion and leave to soften for 5 minutes. Cut the chicken
    into bite-size pieces, then add to the onion and turn
    the heat up to medium. Cook, stirring occasionally, for
    5 minutes.

3   Meanwhile, to make the massaman paste, bash the
    cardamom pods – a pestle and mortar is good for this
    job – to release the seeds, and discard the husks. Use a
    mini-chopper or food processor to blitz all the massaman
    ingredients, including the cardamom seeds, into a paste.
    Add the massaman paste to the chicken, turn the heat up
    to high and cook for 2 minutes, stirring. Remove from the
    heat and set aside.

4   Cut the red pepper into thin slices, slice the spring
    onions and halve the green beans. Heat the remaining
    tablespoon of oil in a second frying pan over a high
    heat and toss in the sliced red pepper, spring onions,
    green beans, rinsed mangetout, julienned carrots and
    whole cherry tomatoes. Cook for 5 minutes, tossing
    occasionally.

5   Put the semi-cooked chicken into a large saucepan and
    add the vegetable stock and coconut milk, mixing well.
    Turn the heat up to high, then add the cooked vegetables
    and the cooked, halved baby potatoes. If necessary, add
    some additional vegetable stock to cover all the chicken
    and vegetables.

6   As soon as the massaman starts to bubble (do not let
    it boil), reduce the heat to a low simmer and leave it
    to finish cooking with the lid on for 20 minutes, stirring
    occasionally. Serve with fluffy boiled rice with a scattering
    of crushed salted peanuts over the top.

Succulent, juicy, finger-licking, sticky sweet duck. Words are, as the man said, not enough. Based in West Cork for the summer months a few years back, I came across Skeaghanore Duck in Brosnan's Spar in Schull. These ducks are hand-reared near Ballydehob in West Cork and have an incredible flavour.

Sticky Sweet Roast Duck Breast

Serves 2

1 plump Skeaghanore duck breast

3 tbsp low-salt soy sauce

3 tbsp orange marmalade (I use Folláin)

Rocket or baby spinach leaves, to serve

1   Preheat a fan oven to 210°C.

2   Heat a heavy-based, dry frying pan on a high heat. Slash the skin of the duck breast, scoring it with lines that criss-cross each other diagonally. Place the duck on the hot pan, skin side down, to sear for 2 minutes. Turn the duck breast over and cook the other side for 2 minutes more.

3   Pour the soy sauce and marmalade into a small roasting tin and mix well. Add the partially cooked duck breast to the roasting tin. Coat it in the sauce and cook in the oven, skin side up, for 10 minutes. Baste with the sauce midway through cooking.

4   Remove the duck breast from the roasting tin and allow it to rest on a board for 5 minutes before cutting it into slices. Serve on a bed of rocket or baby spinach with the marmalade sauce spooned over the top.

Beef Dishes

Beef and Onion Hotpot

Serves 6

4 medium onions

4 shallots (I use banana shallots, but they come in all shapes, sizes and varieties)

50g butter

2–3 tbsp rapeseed or coconut oil

1kg diced stewing beef

A little plain flour, for dusting

250ml vegetable stock

500ml beef stock

4–5 fresh thyme sprigs, plus extra to garnish (or 1 tsp dried thyme)

8–10 medium potatoes

50–75g Cheddar cheese

1   Preheat a fan oven to 160°C.

2   Peel the onions and shallots and slice them into rings. Melt the butter in a large saucepan over a low heat along with 1 tablespoon of oil. Add the onions and shallots. Put a lid on and leave the onions and shallots to sweat for 10 minutes while you prepare the meat.

3   Heat 1 tablespoon of oil in a large frying pan over a medium to high heat. Place the beef in a large bowl and sprinkle with a little flour. Toss the beef in the flour to lightly coat it. Brown the beef in the hot oil in batches – don't overcrowd the pan. You may need to add more oil in between browning batches. Once browned, transfer the beef to a large casserole dish.

4   By now the onions should be well softened, so transfer them to the frying pan that the beef was cooked in and stir them well to scrape up any browned bits from the bottom of the pan. Continue to cook the onions on a high heat until they begin to change colour and are turning golden. Add the onions to the beef in the casserole dish and mix well.

5   Deglaze any remaining sticky bits in the frying pan by adding some of the stock and scraping the bottom of the pan with a wooden spoon. Pour this into the casserole dish along with all the remaining stock and push in a few fresh thyme sprigs. Cover the casserole and cook in the oven for at least 1½ hours and up to 2½ hours if you have time, which will result in more tender beef.

6   Around 40 minutes before the end of the cooking time, scrub the potatoes but leave the skins on. Thinly slice them and boil in a saucepan of water for 5–8 minutes, until they are just starting to turn tender. Drain well. Remove the casserole dish from the oven and arrange the potato slices on top of the beef and onion stew, then grate the Cheddar cheese on top.

7   Return the casserole to the oven, uncovered, and turn up the temperature to 190°C. Cook for a further 20–30 minutes, until the cheese has melted and turned golden brown and the potatoes are cooked through. Garnish with a sprig of thyme and serve straight to the table.

This is an indulgent dinner that deserves time to savour and enjoy it. To up the flavour of the Portobello mushrooms, real Irish butter is mashed with parsley and crushed garlic, with a dollop placed in each mushroom.

Irish Angus Fillet Steaks with Portobello Mushrooms

Serves 2

2 Irish Angus fillet steaks

Small handful of fresh curly parsley

75g real Irish butter, softened

2 garlic cloves

Rapeseed oil

2 large Portobello mushrooms

Crusty bread

Sea salt and freshly ground black pepper

Rocket leaves

Finely chopped fresh chives, to garnish

1 Preheat a fan oven to 200°C.

2 Take the steaks out of the fridge and set aside.

3 Finely chop the parsley, then mix it into the softened butter, using a fork to mash it well.

4 Take 2 teaspoons of the parsley butter and mix it with one crushed garlic clove to make a herby garlic butter for the mushrooms.

5 Put two small drops of oil on a small baking tray and place the upturned Portobello mushrooms (stalks facing up) on the oil on the tray. Place a knob of the herby garlic butter onto each mushroom and cook in the oven for 20 minutes.

6 Meanwhile, cut the remaining garlic clove in half and rub the cut side onto thick-cut slices of crusty bread. Butter the bread with the remaining parsley butter and set aside.

7 When the mushrooms have been cooking for 10 minutes, place the steaks on a plate, drizzle them with a little oil and season with ground sea salt and freshly ground black pepper. Heat a dry non-stick griddle pan or frying pan to high and sear the steaks for 1 minute on each side. Reduce the heat to medium and continue to cook for approximately 2 minutes more on each side for a rare steak. Cook a 3.5cm-thick fillet steak for 2 minutes per side for rare, 3 minutes per side for medium-rare and 4½ minutes per side for medium.

8 Toast the garlic bread under a hot grill for 1–2 minutes, until the butter melts and the edges are getting crispy.

9 Serve the steaks on a bed of rocket leaves with one mushroom each and slices of garlic bread. Spoon some of the garlic butter juices in the mushrooms over the steaks and garnish with finely chopped chives.

This is a gem of a recipe courtesy of Bord Bia (the Irish Food Board) and you can find this and other tasty recipes on their website. It gives great Irish beef a nice warm taste of India and it's a lovely one for the winter months.

Beef Curry with Butternut Squash

Courtesy of Bord Bia

Serves 6

1 butternut squash

1 onion

4 garlic cloves

2 fresh red chillies

4cm chunk of fresh ginger

6 cardamom pods (optional)

2 tbsp coconut or rapeseed oil

1kg lean beef pieces

1½ tbsp ground cumin

1½ tbsp ground coriander

1 tbsp ground cinnamon

1 x 400g tin of chopped tomatoes

200ml beef stock

Zest and juice of 1 lemon (optional)

Chopped fresh coriander or parsley, to garnish

Boiled rice, to serve

Natural yoghurt, to serve

1   Preheat a fan oven to 160°C.

2   Peel the butternut squash, cut it in half and scoop out the seeds, then cut the squash into 2–3cm chunks. Peel and chop the onion and garlic. Deseed and finely chop the chillies. Peel and grate the ginger. Bash the cardamom pods – a pestle and mortar is good for this job – to release the seeds, and discard the husks.

3   Heat the oil in a large, hob-proof casserole dish over a medium to high heat and brown the beef in batches for a couple of minutes. It doesn't have to be completely brown on all sides. You're not cooking the beef in this step, just improving the flavour by searing it.

4   Remove the seared beef to a plate while you cook the chopped onion in the casserole dish for a couple of minutes, adding a little more oil if needed. Stir in the chopped garlic, chillies, ginger, cardamom seeds, cumin, coriander and cinnamon and cook for a couple more minutes. Add the diced butternut squash and stir well to coat with the spices. Stir in the tinned tomatoes and the stock, then return the beef and its juices to the casserole dish.

5   Cover the dish and cook in the oven for 1½ hours, until the beef is tender. Stir in the lemon zest and juice (if using) and sprinkle over some chopped fresh coriander or parsley. Serve with rice and a dollop of natural yoghurt.

Cheat's Wellington with Jameson Jus

Serves 2

2 Irish beef fillet steaks

200g mushrooms

1 medium onion

1 garlic clove

2 tbsp rapeseed

50g salted butter

1 tsp dried thyme

White wine (optional)

2 large puff pastry vol-au-vent cases, frozen

1 egg yolk, beaten

Sea salt and freshly ground black pepper

2 tbsp Jameson whiskey

Fresh flat-leaf parsley, finely chopped, to garnish

1 Preheat a fan oven to 200°C.

2 Take the steaks out of the fridge and set aside.

3 Finely chop the mushrooms and the onion. Peel and crush the garlic. Heat 1 tablespoon of oil in a large frying pan over a low heat. Add the onion and cook for 5 minutes to soften, then add the crushed garlic. Raise the heat to medium and stir to combine for 1 minute, then add the butter. Once the butter has melted, add the mushrooms and dried thyme with a good splash of white wine if you like. Mix well and leave to cook for 20 minutes on a medium heat, stirring occasionally.

4 While the mushrooms are cooking, place a baking tray in the hot oven for 1 minute. Take it out and place the frozen pastry cases on the hot tray. Brush the outer edges of the pastry with the beaten egg yolk. Cook the pastry cases according to the packet instructions, turning the tray halfway through the cooking time.

5 Meanwhile, heat a non-stick griddle pan or frying pan without any oil over a high heat. Place the steaks on a plate, drizzle them with the remaining tablespoon of oil and season with ground sea salt and freshly ground black pepper. As my steaks are generally quite thick, I like to cook them for 3 minutes on each side for medium-rare and then turn them onto the edges to sear the sides, holding them steady with a cooking tongs as I turn them all the way around. Cook a 3.5cm-thick fillet steak for 2 minutes per side for rare, 3 minutes per side for medium-rare and 4½ minutes per side for medium. Once the steaks are cooked, transfer them to a wooden board to rest for at least 5 minutes before slicing, so they stay juicy.

6 Deglaze the steak pan by turning the heat to high and splashing in the Jameson and ½ teaspoon of ground black pepper. Turn the heat off but leave the pan on the hob until you're ready to serve.

7 Once the pastry cases are golden and well risen, remove them from the oven and fill with the mushroom mixture. Serve with sliced fillet steak, a drizzle of Jameson jus and a scattering of finely chopped fresh parsley.

These can be made with varying degrees of spiciness and topped with all sorts of good things like sour cream, grated cheese, jalapeños and guacamole. This is a really quick and tasty supper dish. Once your beef is cooked through, it's merely a help-yourself-at-the-table assembly job. This is a mildly spiced version, but if you want it hotter, put in 1 teaspoon of cayenne pepper and 1 teaspoon of hot chilli powder instead of the paprika and mild chilli powder listed below.

Spicy Beef Fajitas

Serves 4

1 tbsp coconut or rapeseed oil

500g steak mince

1 tsp ground turmeric

½ tsp regular paprika

½ tsp mild chilli powder

140g tomato purée

300ml water

8 small or 4 large flour tortillas

Tomato and coriander salsa (page 125), grated Cheddar cheese, sour cream and rocket leaves, to serve

1 Heat the oil in a large frying pan over a medium to high heat and cook the mince thoroughly. Mix the turmeric, paprika and chilli powder into the cooked mince and cook for 1 minute. Add the tomato purée and cook for 1 minute more. Add half of the water (150ml) and cook for a minute or two, stirring, then stir in the remaining water and heat it through.

2 Heat the flour tortillas in a warm oven or under the grill (they heat well in the microwave too – give them 20 seconds each).

3 Spoon a little salsa onto your fajita, then top with rocket leaves, spicy beef, grated Cheddar and sour cream and wrap it up. Great with a cold beer.

Lamb *Dishes*

Ras el hanout has become a staple in my store cupboard. Wonderfully fragrant and delicately spiced, it won't overpower the palate.

Moroccan Lamb

Serves 6

1 medium onion

1 tbsp rapeseed or coconut oil

500–600g diced stewing lamb

3 garlic cloves

1 tbsp ras el hanout

1 x 400g tin of chopped tomatoes

100ml water

2 tbsp runny honey

Apricot couscous (page 117), to serve

1   Preheat a fan oven to 150°C.

2   Peel and finely chop the onion. Heat the oil in a large, hob-proof casserole dish and gently fry the onion for 5 minutes over a low heat. Raise the heat to medium, push the onion to the sides of the pot, add the diced lamb and brown for 2 minutes. Peel and crush the garlic, then add it to the centre of the pot to cook for 1 minute. Add the ras el hanout and cook for 1 minute before adding the chopped tomatoes, water and honey and mixing well.

3   Cover the casserole dish with a lid and cook in the oven for 1½ hours, until the lamb is tender. Check it after 1 hour, and if there are any signs of it drying out, add some more water. Great with couscous and an easy-to-cook vegetable like broccoli.

When I first cooked this dish I had thought of cutting the apricots into smaller pieces to stretch them further, but when I raised a plumped-up forkful to my mouth, I was glad that I had only cut them in half. It was hard to believe that something once dry could be reconstituted to be so moist, juicy and delicious. This is great served with lemon and coriander couscous.

Ginger and Apricot Lamb Stew

Serves 4

4 tbsp coconut or rapeseed oil

500g stewing lamb pieces

2 onions

2 garlic cloves

Thumb-size piece of fresh ginger

10 soft dried apricots

500ml vegetable stock

2 tbsp tomato purée

4 tsp ras el hanout

Lemon and coriander couscous (page 118), to serve

Lemon wedges, to serve

Fresh coriander leaves, to garnish

1   Heat 2 tablespoons of the oil in a large pan over a medium to high heat and brown the lamb. Meanwhile, peel and thinly slice the onions and peel and chop the garlic and ginger. Once the lamb has been lightly browned, add the remaining 2 tablespoons of oil along with the onions, garlic and ginger. Stir well and cook over a medium heat for 5 minutes.

2   Cut the dried apricots in half and add to the pan along with the vegetable stock, tomato purée and ras el hanout. Simmer gently for 1 hour, until the lamb is tender.

3   Serve with couscous and lemon wedges, and garnish with fresh coriander leaves.

Let summer linger a little longer with this Sicilian-inspired dish. I was lucky enough to taste authentic Parmigiana cooked by my brother-in-law's grandmother in Sicily. Out of all the many, many amazing dishes cooked for us, it was the dish that I most wanted to recreate. I've added lamb to the Parmigiana so that it can feature as a substantial stand-alone dish, one which now gives a distinct nod towards Greek moussaka too. As Parmesan can be quite expensive, feel free to substitute a different cheese, such as a cheaper Grana Padano or Pecorino Romano.

Lamb Parmigiana

Serves 6

Rapeseed oil, for frying and drizzling

500g minced lamb

1 medium onion

2 garlic cloves

2 x 400g tins of chopped tomatoes

2 tsp dried oregano

2 aubergines

50g Parmesan, grated (about half a regular-sized wedge)

Crusty bread, to serve

1   Preheat a fan oven to 180°C.

2   Heat 1 tablespoon of oil in a large pan over a medium heat and brown the minced lamb. While that's cooking, finely chop the onion and peel and crush the garlic. Push the browned mince to the side of the pan, add the chopped onion to the centre and allow it to soften for a few minutes. Add the garlic and cook for 1 minute more before stirring in the chopped tomatoes and oregano. Leave to simmer for 10 minutes, stirring occasionally.

3   Heat 1 tablespoon of oil in another large frying pan or griddle pan over a medium heat. Cut the aubergines into 1cm-thick slices and slightly brown the slices on both sides, drizzling over some extra oil so that they soften a little as they cook. Once browned, remove to a plate lined with kitchen paper to absorb any excess oil. You may need to do this in a couple of batches.

4   Spread a layer of minced lamb in the bottom of a large baking dish and top with a layer of aubergine slices, then a layer of grated Parmesan. Repeat the layers, finishing with a generous topping of grated Parmesan.

5   Bake in the hot oven for about 15 minutes, until the cheese has melted and the meat is bubbling up underneath the aubergines. Enjoy with some crusty bread.

Irish lamb chops have an amazing flavour. I love them really well done with the fat nice and crispy so I can pick them up and chase every last tasty bit, so I actually cook my lamb chops for twice as long as recommended below. I suggest you serve these with some comforting mustardy mash (page 116) or maybe the chickpea salad on page 123.

Rosemary and Lemon Lamb Chops

Serves 2

4 garlic cloves

2 tsp fresh rosemary needles picked from their woody stalks

Zest and juice of ½ lemon

1 tbsp rapeseed oil

4 boneless Irish lamb chops

Mustardy mash (page 116), to serve

Sugar snap peas, to serve

1   Peel and crush the garlic and finely chop the fresh rosemary. Mix them in a small bowl with the lemon zest and juice and the oil to make a marinade. Place the lamb chops in a non-metallic dish and pour over the marinade, turning the chops over to cover both sides. Put in the fridge for a couple of hours or ideally overnight to allow the lamb to absorb the flavours.

2   Heat a heavy-based, non-stick frying pan over a medium heat and cook the chops for 3–4 minutes on each side (you don't need to brush off the marinade). Check that they are cooked through to the middle before serving with mustardy mash and some lightly cooked crunchy greens like sugar snap peas.

Pork Dishes

As a big fan of cranberry sauce, I think it makes an excellent pairing with pork.

Cranberry Pork Chops

Serves 4

1 tbsp rapeseed or coconut oil

4 pork chops

2 medium onions

500ml chicken stock

3 heaped tbsp cranberry sauce

Carrot, parsnip and Bramley apple mash (page 115), to serve

1   Preheat a fan oven to 200°C.

2   Heat the oil in a large frying pan over a high heat and brown the chops on each side for 2 minutes. While the chops are browning, peel and thinly slice the onions.

3   Place the browned chops on a baking tray in the oven to continue cooking.

4   Reduce the hob heat to medium and soften the sliced onions in the frying pan used for the pork, for 5 minutes. Add the chicken stock and cranberry sauce to the onions and mix well. Bring to the boil, then reduce the heat to medium. Return the chops to the pan along with any of their juices in the baking tray and stir through. Serve with the carrot, parsnip and Bramley apple mash.

Simple, tasty and quick. You might find a jar of harissa paste on one of the larger supermarket's shelves, but if not, it will more than likely be waiting amidst a tantalising display of goodies in a specialist food shop or deli. This dish would be great with the Moroccan couscous in my first book, *Gimme the Recipe*, or the pea and mint bulgur wheat salad on page 119.

Harissa Pork Chops

Serves 4

4 pork chops

4 tsp harissa paste

1 Preheat a fan oven to 200°C.

2 Place the pork chops on a baking tray and blob a teaspoon of harissa paste onto each chop. Spread the paste all over the chop with the back of the spoon or a knife, turning them over until both sides have an even coating.

3 Cook in the hot oven for approximately 20 minutes, until the chops are nicely coloured and cooked through.

Sticky, sweet honey-glazed rashers sit on a bed of couscous fortified with a selection of healthy vegetables. Served hot, this makes a satisfying main and any leftovers are flavoursome enough to be welcomed cold in a lunch box or as a side dish served with a juicy burger.

Honey-Glazed Rashers with Lemon and Vegetable Couscous

Serves 4

1 medium red onion

1 yellow pepper

1 red pepper

1 aubergine

1 courgette

3 tbsp rapeseed oil

8 rashers of bacon

1 tbsp runny honey

For the couscous

1 tbsp butter

250g couscous

250ml hot vegetable stock

1 lemon

Small bunch of fresh coriander, roughly chopped

1 Peel the red onion and cut into bite-size chunks. Deseed the peppers and chop into bite-size chunks. Slice both the aubergine and courgette into four lengthways, then chop each length into bite-size chunks. Put the chopped vegetables in a large bowl, drizzle in 2 tablespoons of the oil and mix well.

2 Heat a large griddle or frying pan and cook the oiled vegetables for 5–8 minutes over a medium heat, mixing and tossing the vegetables occasionally as they cook.

3 Meanwhile, prepare the couscous by melting the butter in a medium saucepan over a medium heat. Add the couscous, stir well and cook for 1–2 minutes. Take the couscous off the heat and pour in the hot vegetable stock. Cover the pan with a lid and leave to stand for 5 minutes. Check on the vegetables while you prepare the couscous – you want them to retain a bit of bite, so if they're getting too soft, take the pan off the heat.

4 Heat the remaining tablespoon of oil in a frying pan and cook the rashers on a high heat on one side until they are beginning to brown, then turn them over and drizzle the browned side with honey. Reduce the heat to low to finish cooking the other side for a couple of minutes.

5 Take the lid off the couscous and use a fork to fluff up the grains. Zest the lemon first, then juice it. Add the zest and juice to the couscous and stir well. Add the chopped fresh coriander and stir it through.

6 Place the cooked vegetables in a large serving bowl and stir in the lemony couscous. Serve straight from the bowl with the honey-glazed rashers on top.

You may be somewhat sick of cooking pasta dishes and speedy suppers that are met with an 'oh no, not pasta again' from the choir of resident critics. This is, however, a tasty, grown-up dish and I do hope you'll enjoy it. Conchiglie pasta is the shell-shaped pasta like the magical conch that you'll find on the beach and can hear the sea from.

Conchiglie Pasta with Courgettes and Bacon

Serves 4

300g pasta shells (conchiglie)

1 tbsp rapeseed oil

6 rashers of bacon

100g sun-dried tomatoes preserved in oil

2 tsp balsamic vinegar

2 courgettes

4 tbsp crème fraîche

1 tbsp semi-sun-dried tomato pesto

Fresh flat-leaf parsley, chopped, to garnish

Parmesan, to garnish (optional)

1 Bring a large saucepan of salted water to the boil for the pasta. Cook the pasta shells according to the packet instructions, stirring frequently.

2 Meanwhile, heat the oil in a large frying pan. Roughly chop the rashers and cook them over a medium to high heat. Once the rashers have begun to brown and crisp, push them to the side of the pan. Roughly chop the sun-dried tomatoes and place them in the centre of the frying pan. Drizzle the balsamic vinegar on top of the tomatoes and stir them around a little as they cook for a couple of minutes.

3 Cut the courgettes into thick slices. Push the tomatoes out to the side of the pan and fry the courgette slices for 1 minute on each side – you may need to add more oil.

4 When it's cooked, drain the pasta and drizzle with a little oil to prevent it from sticking.

5 Mix the crème fraîche and the sun-dried tomato pesto into the bacon, sun-dried tomatoes and courgettes, cooking until it's just heated through.

6 Serve bowls of pasta shells topped with the creamy bacon, tomato and courgette sauce and garnish generously with chopped fresh parsley.

In my opinion, quesadillas rank up there with omelettes as the perfect standby. Breakfast, lunch, dinner or a snack, quesadillas can be anything you want them to be. When I'm in West Cork I love to have this version with blackberry and apple chutney and some local Gubbeen cheese and bacon.

Bacon, Cheese and Chutney Quesadilla

Serves 1 hungry person or stretch it to 2 served with a side salad

A little coconut or rapeseed oil, for frying

3 rashers of bacon

2 flour tortillas

Blackberry and apple chutney (page 149) or any other chutney

Handful of your favourite grated cheese (I like to use Gubbeen or Durrus semi-soft)

1   Heat a little oil in a large frying pan. Roughly chop the rashers and cook them over a medium to high heat until they have begun to brown and crisp up.

2   Generously smear one side of a tortilla with chutney. Top the chutney with the cooked rashers and then the grated cheese. Place the second tortilla on top and press down to sandwich it together.

3   Cook the quesadilla in the frying pan you used to fry the rashers. Fry on each side until golden brown. Allow to stand for a few minutes before cutting into wedges to serve.

I spent many summers in Northern Ireland on my grandparents' farm, and some mornings my grandmother would pull out her griddle pan and make these potato farls as part of an Ulster fry. I like to have them from time to time as a simple yet indulgent supper. Cooked in bacon fat, these are not for the faint-hearted, but if you lead a fairly healthy lifestyle most of the time, then I think it's essential that you have an occasional blow-out and you should experience homemade potato farls at least once. Other than their shape, these farls bear little resemblance to the ones you'll find on the shelf of a supermarket. This recipe makes eight farls, and one or two per person is generally plenty. Any leftovers will reheat well when fried again.

Potato Farls with Crispy Rashers

Serves 4

1kg potatoes (approx. 5 medium-sized potatoes)

1 tbsp rapeseed oil

8 rashers of bacon

30g butter

Good pinch of salt

100g plain flour, plus extra for dusting

Ketchup, to serve

Fresh flat-leaf parsley, chopped, to garnish

1 Peel the potatoes and cook them in a saucepan of boiling water for 20 minutes or so, until tender (or cut the potatoes into smaller pieces for a quicker cooking time if you prefer).

2 While the potatoes are cooking, heat the oil in a large frying pan and cook the rashers on a high heat on one side until they are beginning to brown, then turn them over and reduce the heat to low to finish cooking the other side for a couple of minutes. Keep them warm in a warm oven until the potato farls are cooked and leave the bacon fat in the pan to fry the farls in later.

3 Drain the potatoes well, then place them in a large bowl and mash with the butter and a good pinch of salt. Leave to cool for 5 minutes, then use a fork to mix in the flour.

4 Lightly dust the worktop and your hands with flour. Using your floured hands, tip the mashed potatoes out of the bowl and roll into a large ball. Cut the ball in half.

5 Shape one half into a smaller ball and use your hands to flatten it out into a circle on the floured worktop. Cut the circle into four triangular wedges (farls). Do the same with the second ball so that you end up with eight farls.

6 Heat the bacon fat that remains in the large frying pan you used earlier over a medium to high heat. Cook the farls, four at a time, for 3 minutes on each side, until they are golden brown.

7 Serve the farls warm with the crispy rashers, ketchup and a little chopped fresh parsley to garnish.

My mother's version of champ potatoes was often enjoyed in a heaped mound surrounded by a moat of Bisto gravy and usually accompanied by sausages and peas. Creamy mashed potatoes mixed with butter and milk and lots of chopped spring onions is a simple supper that's perfect for a cold winter evening, but instead of sausages I like to use a West Cork white pudding accompanied by champ and a side of pea and parsley purée. I serve this with a simple dollop of lemon and parsley crème fraîche on the side, which gives the dish a nice zingy twist.

White Pudding with Pea Purée and Champ

Serves 4

300g traditional white pudding

1 tbsp rapeseed or coconut oil

For the champ

8–10 medium potatoes

Large knob of butter

Splash of milk, to mash

3–4 spring onions, chopped

For the pea purée

300g frozen peas

1 tbsp crème fraîche

1 tbsp chopped fresh flat-leaf parsley

For the zingy crème fraîche

4 tbsp crème fraîche

1 tbsp chopped fresh flat-leaf parsley

Zest of 1 lemon

1   Peel the potatoes and boil them for 20 minutes or so, until they are tender enough to mash. Drain well.

2   While the potatoes are boiling, slice the pudding lengthways into four long slices. Heat the oil in a large frying pan over a medium heat and cook the pudding until it's golden on both sides.

3   Cook the frozen peas in boiling water, then drain and blitz in a food processor or mini-chopper with 1 tablespoon of crème fraîche and 1 tablespoon of chopped fresh parsley. Don't over-process it, though, as you want it to have a little bit of texture.

4   Make the zingy crème fraîche by mixing the 4 tablespoons of crème fraîche with 1 tablespoon of parsley and the lemon zest.

5   Mash the potatoes with plenty of butter and milk, then stir in the chopped spring onions.

6   Cut the four lengths of cooked white pudding in half. Serve two pieces each on a bed of champ with a side of the pea purée and a dollop of zingy crème fraîche.

Plain pork ribs can be hard to get a hold of. You are unlikely to find them in your supermarket, so support your local butcher by ordering some there. Smoked paprika should be readily available, though, and the key to the sweet stickiness of these ribs is adding the honey towards the very end of the cooking time.

Sticky BBQ Ribs

Serves 4

250g tomato passata

2 garlic cloves, crushed

4 tbsp dark brown muscovado sugar

3 tbsp smoked paprika

2 tbsp balsamic vinegar

1 tbsp rapeseed oil

1 tbsp Worcestershire sauce

2 racks of pork ribs (approx. 1kg in total)

3 tbsp runny honey

1   Place all the ingredients apart from the pork ribs and honey into a medium-sized saucepan. Stir them together and bring to the boil, then reduce to a simmer for 30 minutes.

2   Preheat a fan oven to 160°C.

3   Place the ribs onto a large foil-lined baking tray and pour over the BBQ sauce, using your hands to coat the ribs well on all sides. Cover the baking tray with tinfoil and cook for 1½ hours.

4   Remove the tray from the oven and remove the foil. Raise the oven temperature to 200°C and return the ribs to the oven for 10 minutes. Remove the tray again, drizzle the honey over the ribs and return to the oven for a further 10 minutes, until the ribs are glazed and sticky.

There is a lot of to-do in relation to making risotto and there needn't be. This dish is ready to serve in 30 minutes and is a complete meal. There aren't too many dinners that can be whipped up in that amount of time, and I find the stirring and ladling therapeutic. There was no clanging of pans or spitting grease, just a nice, sedate, one-pot experience.

Risotto with Bacon, Peas and Parsley

Serves 4

50g frozen petits pois

4 shallots

1 garlic clove

1 tbsp coconut or rapeseed oil

100g streaky bacon

225g Arborio risotto rice

100ml dry white wine

850ml hot vegetable stock

2 tbsp grated Parmesan

2 tbsp chopped fresh flat-leaf parsley

1   Put the frozen petits pois on a large plate and they will be defrosted by the time you need to use them. Peel, halve and finely slice the shallots. Peel and crush the garlic.

2   Heat the oil in a large frying pan on a medium heat. Use a kitchen scissors to snip in the streaky bacon and cook it for 1 minute. Add the risotto rice and cook for 2–3 minutes, stirring all the time. Don't brown it – lower the heat if you need to. Add the shallots and garlic, stir well and cook for 1 minute. Add the white wine and let it cook for 1 minute. It should bubble – if it doesn't, raise the heat in order to cook off the alcohol.

3   Add two ladles of hot stock to the rice and stir well. When the stock gets absorbed, add another ladle of stock. Continue in this manner until all the stock has been added. This will take 20–25 minutes, stirring every so often.

4   Finally, stir in the thawed peas, the grated Parmesan and the chopped parsley and heat through.

Fish *Dishes*

Fish can be quite expensive – a fillet of sea bass is twice the price of a chicken fillet and comes in at under half the weight, so it's not something I'd want to waste on a picky child. This recipe is absolutely perfect for no-hassle entertaining. Just make sure you've no picky adults attending! It's a complete meal steamed in individual parcels of baking paper that needs to be served straight from the oven.

Sea Bass Parcels

Serves 4

250g baby potatoes

4 sea bass fillets

100g slow-roasted cherry tomatoes (you can find these at deli counters or you can just use regular sun-dried tomatoes), drained and chopped

100g fine green beans

4 spring onions

4 tbsp Sauvignon Blanc or any white wine that you like to drink

1   Preheat a fan oven to 200°C. Cut out four 30cm square sheets of baking paper.

2   Par-cook the baby potatoes, skin on, in the microwave for 4 minutes and set aside.

3   Place the four sheets of paper on the worktop and place a sea bass fillet in the centre of each one. Slice the baby potatoes and place equal portions close along one side of the sea bass in each packet. Scatter equal portions of the drained, chopped slow-roasted cherry tomatoes over the potatoes. Halve the fine green beans and finely chop the spring onions and scatter equal portions on top of the sea bass fillets. Pour 1 tablespoon of white wine over each fillet.

4   Fold the edges of the paper in by 1cm all round to stiffen the paper. It should still be a large square. Bring in the two opposite sides to meet and fold them together, then fold in the top and bottom ends. You want a little room in the package for steam to circulate but not escape. Place the parcels onto two baking trays, two parcels per tray.

5   Cook in the hot oven for 10 minutes, then swap shelves and turn the trays around and cook for 5 minutes more. Bring the parcels straight to the table for your guests to open themselves.

Who doesn't love fish and chips, especially as a weekend treat and particularly if the fish is battered? Here's my grown-up version with meaty, chunky monkfish, but instead of being battered it's coated in spiced flour and crunchy breadcrumbs. I like to use wholewheat bread for extra colour, texture and flavour.

Polenta chips make a great alternative to potatoes, though I can't see that they'd be any healthier, really, as they're brushed with oil. Adding cumin and red chilli lends a little heat and I like to serve these with a quick, zesty crème fraîche tartare sauce.

This recipe should be read through carefully before beginning, as there are a number of stages to it.

Spiced Monkfish Goujons with Chunky Cumin and Chilli Polenta Chips

Serves 4

For the polenta chips

Rapeseed oil • 1 litre water

250g polenta • 2 tsp ground cumin

2 tsp red chilli paste or chilli powder

50g grated Cheddar cheese

For the monkfish goujons

3 slices of multigrain wholewheat bread (approx. 170g)

3 heaped tbsp plain flour • 2 tsp ground cumin

2 tsp ground coriander • 1 tsp salt

½ tsp freshly ground black pepper • 2 eggs

750g monkfish tail, skinned and cut into 7.5cm chunks
(ask your fishmonger to do this)

Rapeseed oil, for greasing • Lemon wedges, to serve

For the crème fraîche tartare sauce

6 tbsp crème fraîche • 3 tbsp drained capers

Zest and juice of ½ lemon

Note on timings

You need to prepare the polenta first, as it will need to cool and set for at least 1 hour before cutting into chips and cooking. Put the prepared polenta chips on to begin cooking, then prepare the fish and cook it with the chips for the last 15 minutes.

For the chips

1   To make the polenta chips, oil a small baking tray (approx. 30cm x 20cm) and bring the water to the boil in a saucepan. Whisk in the polenta, cumin and chilli paste. Keep whisking steadily over a high heat as it starts to thicken up, then reduce the heat and continue whisking for a couple of minutes, until it's smooth and thick. You want it to be a blobbing consistency so that when you place it on the tray it won't run. Take the pan off the heat and whisk in the grated cheese. Pour the thick polenta into the oiled baking tray, spreading it evenly with a spatula, and leave it in a cool, dry place for 1–2 hours, until set.

2   Preheat a fan oven to 220°C. Oil a large baking tray (approx. 35cm x 40cm).

3   Tip the tray of set polenta upside down onto the larger tray and give it a few taps so that the polenta falls out onto the larger tray. Cut the set polenta into chunky chips sized to your liking, then space them out on the tray and use a pastry brush to oil them on all sides.

4   Cook the chips in the hot oven for about 35 minutes, until golden brown and nicely crisped up on the outside, turning the heat down to 200°C for the last 5 minutes.

For the fish and sauce

1   Prepare the monkfish goujons as soon as the polenta chips go into the oven so that they can cook with them for the last 15 minutes.

2   Use a mini-chopper or food processor to make the bread into breadcrumbs and set on a large plate. Place the flour, cumin, coriander, salt and pepper onto another large plate and mix together with a fork. Beat the eggs in a shallow, wide-rimmed bowl.

3   Taking individual chunks of monkfish one at a time, first dip them in the beaten egg, then coat in the spiced flour, then dip in the egg again and coat in breadcrumbs. Set the breaded goujon aside and repeat for the remaining fish.

4   Place two baking trays in the hot oven for just 1 minute. Remove the trays from the oven and brush with some rapeseed oil, then place the breaded monkfish on the hot oiled trays. Cook in the oven for 10 minutes, then reduce the heat to 200°C and cook for a further 5 minutes. Remove and check the core temperature – it should be piping hot.

5   While the fish is cooking, make the zesty crème fraîche tartare sauce by blitzing the crème fraîche, drained capers and lemon juice in a mini-chopper. Spoon into a small serving bowl and sprinkle with the lemon zest.

6   Serve the monkfish goujons with the chunky polenta chips, tartare sauce and lemon wedges on the side.

Salads and Sides

Sweet potato and carrot work really well together. I often just mash them with some chopped fresh coriander and butter, but I have also concocted this sweet and spicy chilli-based mixture to mash into them, and it makes for a lovely side dish. It's terrific served with a paprika spiced roast chicken. I like to purée this, but you can just roughly mash it if you prefer.

Spicy Sweet Potato and Carrot Mash

Serves 6

750g sweet potatoes (approx. 6 small or 2 large)

500g carrots (approx. 4 large)

2 tbsp rapeseed or coconut oil

2 tbsp dark brown sugar

1 fresh red chilli, deseeded and finely chopped

2 tbsp apple cider vinegar

2 tbsp water

1   Peel the sweet potatoes and cut them into 2.5cm chunks and peel and slice the carrots. Boil them together in a saucepan of water until they're tender enough to mash, which will take 15–20 minutes.

2   Meanwhile, heat the oil in a small saucepan over a medium heat, then stir in the brown sugar until it has dissolved into a paste. Add the finely chopped red chilli, the cider vinegar and the water. Stir well and bring to the boil, then reduce to a simmer for 5 minutes.

3   Add half of the chilli mixture to the cooked and drained sweet potato and carrots in a large bowl and begin to mash them together (or purée with a food processor if you prefer). Add as much of the remaining chilli mixture as you need to bring it to your desired consistency as you continue to mash or purée. You might not need to add all the chilli mixture – sometimes it can get too sloppy if you add it all.

Carrot and parsnip mash is a favourite of my dad's from his childhood. The inherent sweetness of the veg lends itself well to the addition of Bramley apples. Any leftovers are excellent shaped into small vegetable patties and fried.

Carrot, Parsnip and Bramley Apple Mash

Serves 4

4 medium carrots

1 medium parsnip

1 medium Bramley apple

A little butter, for mashing

1   Peel and chop the carrots and parsnip. Boil the carrots on their own for 10 minutes before adding the parsnip and boiling for a further 5 minutes, until both are tender enough to mash.

2   While the vegetables are boiling, peel, core and chop the Bramley apple into chunks and cook in a small saucepan with a tiny splash of water over a medium heat, until it's beginning to soften but still retains a little texture.

3   Combine the cooked carrots, parsnips and Bramley apple with a little butter in a large bowl and mash well.

This recipe originates from a hospital waiting room magazine. Who knows what limb was about to be X-rayed, I just know it wasn't one of mine! Delicious, creamy and tasty, this is comfort defined, and with two lines of instructions, it couldn't be simpler. This is a great side dish, and I would happily eat the lot on its own.

Mustardy Mash

Serves 4

750g potatoes

100ml milk

4 tbsp soft cheese (I use Ardsallagh goats' cheese)

1 tbsp wholegrain mustard

Salt and freshly ground black pepper

Knob of butter

1 Boil the potatoes until they're tender, then peel and mash them with the milk, cheese and mustard. Serve large dollops of mustardy mash seasoned with salt and pepper and a knob of butter.

Dried apricots are another one of those ingredients that like to hang about in the cupboard waiting to be used up. I love how dried apricots can spring to life and plump up when given a bit of heat and they add a surprise pop of sweetness in savoury dishes. This couscous is good served hot or cold.

Apricot Couscous

Serves 4–6

1 tbsp butter

250g couscous

250ml hot chicken stock (from a cube is fine)

Handful of dried apricots

1 tbsp rapeseed or coconut oil

2 tbsp water

1 tbsp apricot jam

Handful of fresh flat-leaf parsley

1   Melt the butter in a saucepan over a medium heat, then add the couscous and cook for 1 minute, stirring. Remove the pan from the heat, pour in the hot chicken stock and cover with a lid or cling film. Leave to stand for 5 minutes.

2   Meanwhile, finely chop the dried apricots. Heat the oil in a small frying pan and heat the chopped dried apricots in the pan with the water and apricot jam over a medium heat for a few minutes, until the apricots plump up.

3   Finely chop the fresh parsley. Remove the lid from the couscous and use a fork to fluff it up before mixing in the apricots and parsley.

Fresh coriander is one of those herbs that you either love or despise. It's got such a strong, heady fragrance, especially when you cut into it. Personally, I can't get enough of it and I do hope you love it too. Adding lemon juice to couscous is so simple, yet it instantly elevates it from bland to sensational, making this an easy but super-tasty dish.

Lemon and Coriander Couscous

Serves 4–6

1 tbsp butter

250g couscous

250ml hot chicken stock (from a cube is fine)

Small handful of fresh coriander

Juice of 1 lemon

1 Melt the butter in a saucepan over a medium heat, then add the couscous and cook for 1 minute, stirring. Remove the pan from the heat, pour in the hot chicken stock and cover with a lid or cling film. Leave to stand for 5 minutes.

2 Finely chop the fresh coriander. Remove the lid from the couscous and use a fork to fluff it up before mixing in the lemon juice and coriander. Stir well and serve.

This is a simple and tasty side dish that I like to serve with fried lamb chops or on its own for a super-healthy lunch. It marries the classic combination of mint and peas and is a Middle Eastern tabbouleh-influenced bulgur wheat salad.

Pea and Mint Bulgur Wheat Salad

Serves 4

225g petit pois or any frozen peas

200g bulgur wheat

225ml hot chicken stock

Big handful of fresh flat-leaf parsley

4 fresh mint leaves

4 spring onions

Juice of 1 lemon

1   Put the peas in a saucepan and cover them with boiling water. Bring to the boil and cook according to the packet instructions, then drain.

2   Place the bulgur wheat in a medium-sized heatproof bowl, pour over the hot chicken stock and cover with cling film (or a plate) for about 5 minutes, until all the stock has been absorbed.

3   Finely chop the parsley and mint (you could use a food processor for this) and place in a large serving bowl. Chop the spring onions and mix them through.

4   Fluff up the bulgur wheat with a fork before mixing it through the herbs and spring onions. Add the drained cooked peas and the lemon juice and mix well. Serve while it's still warm as a side dish with cooked meat or serve it cold as a salad.

This is what I'm all about – tasty food that's easy to make and with ingredients that are easily obtainable from your supermarket. Tinned beans are a superb standby and I highly recommend stocking up on a few different varieties. If these are in your store cupboard and you've got a jar of pesto in your fridge, then you're always within reach of a tasty and nutritious lunch. I've upped the flavour stakes with cherry tomatoes that are bursting out of their skins with goodness and griddled courgette ribbons that are quick and easy to prepare.

Cannellini Bean, Roast Cherry Tomato and Griddled Courgette Salad

Serves 4

250g cherry tomatoes

Rapeseed oil

2 courgettes

1 x 400g tin of cannellini beans

2 tbsp basil pesto

1   Preheat a fan oven to 200°C.

2   Place the washed cherry tomatoes on a baking tray, drizzle with a little rapeseed oil and roast in the oven for 10–15 minutes, until they are beginning to burst their skins.

3   Meanwhile, use a speed peeler or a cheese slicer to make courgette strips or ribbons. Heat a splash of oil in a large griddle pan or frying pan on a medium to high heat. Quickly fry the courgettes to lightly brown each side. Set aside on a plate lined with kitchen paper to absorb any excess oil.

4   Drain and rinse the cannellini beans under cold running water, then place in a serving bowl and gently mix in the basil pesto. Stir through the cherry tomatoes and courgette ribbons and serve.

Sweet red pepper, zingy red onion and chickpeas combine with salad leaves to make for a balanced, lightweight summer salad. I like to serve this with a simple paprika-spiced pork or lamb chop or the harissa pork chops on page 90.

Chickpea Salad

Serves 4

1 red onion

1 red pepper

Mixed salad leaves

1 x 400g tin of chickpeas

2 tbsp rapeseed oil

1 tbsp red wine vinegar

1   Finely slice the red onion, deseed and finely slice the red pepper and toss them in a bowl with the salad leaves.

2   Drain and rinse the chickpeas, then add them to the salad.

3   Whisk the oil and vinegar together in a separate small bowl and pour this dressing over the salad, mixing it through the leaves.

This delicious Asian-inspired slaw will keep for a couple of days. I wouldn't attempt to make this without a food processor with a grater attachment or a willing volunteer to grate the carrots!

Carrot and Toasted Sesame Slaw

Serves 4

5 medium carrots

1 medium white onion

2 tbsp sesame seeds

Red wine vinegar

Toasted sesame oil

Sweet chilli sauce

1   Grate the carrots and onion and mix them together in a large bowl.

2   Dry fry the sesame seeds in a small frying pan over a high heat until lightly toasted, then mix into the carrots and onions.

3   Add a good splash of red wine vinegar, a little toasted sesame oil and some sweet chilli sauce. Mix well, taste and adjust the dressing to your liking.

In the summertime I'm inclined to buy more fresh herbs to garnish meals with, which often leads to a pile-up of basil and coriander leaves in the fridge. As they don't last long, I like to use them up in pesto or in a salsa. This salsa is great with the spicy beef fajitas on page 79.

Tomato and Coriander Salsa

Serves 4

250g cherry tomatoes

4 spring onions

1 fresh red chilli

1 bunch of fresh coriander

1 Cut the cherry tomatoes in half and slice the spring onions. Deseed and finely chop the red chilli. Rinse the coriander leaves and roughly chop them. Combine everything in a bowl and mix well. The flavour is best if the salsa is allowed to sit for 30 minutes at room temperature.

I spied a box of freekeh in my local SuperValu and just had to try it. So what is it? The box says: 'High in protein and fibre, greenwheat freekeh is a nutritious toasted grain that makes a wholesome alternative to rice and couscous.' There you have it.

Freekeh Salad with Beetroot and Feta

Serves 4

100g greenwheat freekeh

500ml water

1 tbsp rapeseed oil

1 tsp salt

2 small cooked beetroots (I buy mine pre-cooked and vac-packed)

1 block of feta cheese

Chopped fresh flat-leaf parsley, to serve

1   Put the freekeh and water into a saucepan with the rapeseed oil and salt. Stir and bring to the boil, then reduce the heat and simmer for 15 minutes, until the freekeh is tender. Drain off any excess water and transfer the freekeh to a bowl.

2   Chop the beetroot and cube the feta, then add both to the freekeh. Serve with a scattering of chopped parsley. This is good hot or cold.

This is one of my 'stop food waste' salads that makes use of leftover cooked potatoes and the oft-discarded parsley stalk. When they are snipped very finely, they bring all of their goodness and a lovely crunchy texture.

Parsley Stalk Potato Salad

Cooked potatoes (leftover peeled, cold potatoes are ideal)

Extra virgin rapeseed oil

Mayonnaise

Parsley stalks

Salt and freshly ground black pepper

1   Mash the peeled, cooked potatoes with a little oil and a good bit of mayonnaise. The amount of oil and mayo you need depends on how much potato you have, so use your judgement to create a nice smooth mash.

2   Use a kitchen scissors to finely snip the parsley stalks into tiny pieces and mix them in well with the potatoes. Season with salt and pepper.

For an evening when you don't want to cook and all you really want is a bag of chips but you can't be bothered to go out to the chipper. Great with a box set and some wine.

Quick Spicy Crushed Baby Potatoes

Baby potatoes

Large knob of butter

2 tsp chilli flakes

½ tsp garlic granules

1 Microwave the baby potatoes, skin on, with a splash of water for about 8 minutes, until tender.

2 Melt a large knob of butter in a small saucepan over a low heat. Add the chilli flakes and garlic granules and cook for 1 minute, then add the cooked baby potatoes. Stir until the potatoes are all coated with butter, then lightly crush them with a potato masher.

3 Serve with some greens if you're a health nut, otherwise lash on the salt or some finely grated Parmesan and indulge in front of the telly.

A great side dish to almost anything, these are handy if you're cooking something in the oven anyway, as these will roast away, tastily taking care of themselves.

Paprika Roast Baby Potatoes

Baby potatoes

Rapeseed oil

Regular paprika

Sea salt and freshly ground black pepper

1   Preheat a fan oven to 200°C.

2   Place the baby potatoes on a baking tray and drizzle generously with oil. Use your hands to roll the potatoes around to coat them thoroughly with the oil. Sprinkle over some paprika and season with some crushed sea salt and freshly ground black pepper. Roast for 15–20 minutes, until a knife slips through easily.

Have the easiest dinner party ever by simply assembling a selection of tasty bites. Create something visually stunning by using large bread boards or a black slate and let loose your inner Van Gogh to arrange various tasty morsels to be as appealing as they can be. Make your dips the day before and the only cooking you will have to do will be the pita chips and crostini.

Tapas / Antipasti Board

Olives

Salami slices

Parma ham slices

Melon pieces (use a melon baller for prettiness)

Carrot sticks

Feta cheese cubes

Semi-sun-dried tomatoes

Cooked artichoke hearts

Roast aubergine dip (page 142)

Pea and garlic crostini (page 134)

Paprika pita chips (page 139)

Harissa hummus (page 138)

Selection of Irish farmhouse cheeses

Crusty bread

1 Use ramekins for the dips and all the various bits and pieces and arrange on large boards alongside some great Irish cheeses and crusty bread.

2 You could assemble some of the Parma with melon on cocktail sticks, and maybe feta cubes with semi-sun-dried tomato and a little artichoke heart on cocktail sticks too if you have time. You should only need some extra cocktail sticks and napkins for self-service, making this the easiest entertaining ever.

These crostini are great for entertaining, as you could get ahead and make the pea and mint purée early in the day and keep it refrigerated to create the crostini when needed. Garden peas have a lovely sweetness to them and always work well with fresh mint. Here I've blitzed them with some softened shallots, garlic and rapeseed oil to create a fragrant purée that's delicious on crostini or would be great as a side dish with some lamb kebabs.

This is a simple summery dish that is best eaten in a sunshine-filled garden accompanied by a glass of something cold.

Pea and Garlic Crostini

Serves 4

1 baguette

200g frozen garden peas

50g butter

2 small shallots

1 garlic clove

1 tbsp extra virgin rapeseed oil, plus extra for drizzling on the bread

1 tsp chopped fresh mint (3–4 leaves)

2 small radishes, thinly sliced

1. Preheat a fan oven to 200°C.

2. Slice the baguette and place on a baking tray. Put the bread in the oven for about 5 minutes to crisp up.

3. Bring the peas to the boil in a saucepan of water for 3 minutes, then drain.

4. Melt the butter in a small frying pan over a low to medium heat. Peel and finely slice the shallots, then add to the pan to soften for 5 minutes. Peel and crush the garlic and add to the softened shallots. Add the drained peas to the shallots and garlic and cook for 1 minute, mixing well.

5. Blitz the peas, shallots and garlic in a food processor with the extra virgin rapeseed oil and chopped fresh mint.

6. Drizzle some oil over the crisped baguette slices and return to the oven for 1 minute. Spread the pea and garlic purée on top of the crostini and garnish with some thin slices of radish.

How often do you hear that good food means good ingredients? We know it's true. Take good-quality ingredients, do very little to them and you will be utterly satisfied. These goats' cheese crostini are a prime example of that. They are a superb lunch, or take the portion size down a little to serve as canapés or a starter.

Goats' Cheese Crostini

Crusty bread or baguette slices

Good-quality extra virgin rapeseed oil

Good-quality goats' cheese

Rocket leaves

Balsamic vinegar

Red onion marmalade or caramelised red onion relish (page 150)

1 Lightly toast the bread under the grill. Drizzle a little rapeseed oil on the toasted bread and grill for a further minute. Place a slice of goats' cheese on the toasted bread and grill just until it's beginning to melt and bubble.

2 Arrange some rocket leaves on a plate or serving platter and drizzle with a little rapeseed oil and balsamic vinegar. Serve the goats' cheese crostini on the bed of leaves topped with a little red onion marmalade or relish.

Dips

Summertime means that after a long day's work there are still daylight hours in which you can hopefully sit outside and enjoy some lingering sunlight and warmth. What better way to do this than with a glass of wine in one hand and something tasty to nibble on in the other? This super-fast harissa hummus is the perfect accompaniment to that well-earned tipple.

Harissa Hummus

Makes 1 small bowl

1 x 400g tin of chickpeas

2 garlic cloves, peeled

1 tbsp rapeseed oil

1 tbsp harissa paste

1 tbsp tomato purée

1   Drain and rinse the chickpeas and place in a food processor with all the other ingredients. Blitz to your desired degree of smoothness. This is lovely served with the paprika pita chips opposite or any dipping chips.

These work well with all kinds of dips, and if you make them really small you can even substitute them for croutons to garnish a soup or salad. You could also do the same thing with leftover flour tortillas, but be careful as they crisp up extremely quickly, so reduce the cooking time and keep a close eye on them.

Paprika Pita Chips

4 pita breads

Rapeseed oil

Regular paprika

1   Preheat a fan oven to 200°C.

2   Use a kitchen scissors to cut the pita breads into dip-sized triangular chips. Scatter the chips on a baking tray, drizzle with rapeseed oil and sprinkle with paprika. Toast in the hot oven for 8–10 minutes, until they are nicely coloured and crispy. These chips are best served hot.

Simple, simple, simple, plus healthy and tasty. This dip is made with only two ingredients and is great served with any dipping chips you can get your hands on or even some good crusty bread. I often have leftover pita breads that haven't been used for school lunches and the homemade paprika pita chips on page 139 have a lovely crunch that makes them a perfect accompaniment to this creamy dip.

Roast Aubergine Dip
Makes 1 small bowl

2 aubergines

1 tbsp sun-dried tomato pesto

Paprika pita chips (page 139), to serve

1 Preheat a fan oven to 200°C.

2 Place the whole aubergines straight onto an oven rack. Leave to roast for about 20 minutes, until the aubergines are charring on the outside and tender when pierced with a knife.

3 Remove the skins from the aubergine – they will peel off very easily, but be careful you don't burn yourself – and squeeze away any excess moisture from the pulp. Blitz the aubergine flesh in a food processor along with the tablespoon of sun-dried tomato pesto until smooth. Spoon into a bowl and serve with paprika pita chips.

If in springtime you take some mad notion to grow your own greens, you may end up, as I did, with a glut of lettuce. What to do? Lettuce pesto. Sounds yeuch, but it's actually rather good. It's also the perfect way to use up that waning bag of lettuce leaves in the fridge instead of binning it. Use this pesto as you would any other, to spruce up a sandwich, etc. It's also perfect in the fusilli summer chicken on page 48 or in a quesadilla.

Lettuce Pesto

Makes 1 ramekin

50g pine nuts

50g Parmesan

2 garlic cloves

½ head butter leaf lettuce, washed (or any lettuce leaves)

Small handful of fresh flat-leaf parsley

200ml rapeseed oil

1   Dry fry the pine nuts in a non-stick pan over a medium heat until they are lightly toasted (take care, as they burn easily).

2   Grate the Parmesan and peel and crush the garlic. Roughly chop the lettuce leaves and the parsley.

3   Place everything in a food processor, pour in the oil and blend to your desired consistency, adding more oil if you prefer it runnier. Stored in the fridge in a sterilised glass jar, this should keep well for at least a week.

Salmoriglio? So what's that then, you may well ask. It's a sauce with origins in Sicily that is superb drizzled over barbecued meats. It's punchy and tangy, made with strong, fragrant herbs and given lots of zip with lemon juice and garlic. Source a very good-quality extra virgin olive oil for this, and if you can get one that already has garlic added, all the better.

Salmoriglio

Makes 1 ramekin

2 tbsp fresh thyme leaves (or oregano or marjoram)

Handful of fresh flat-leaf parsley leaves

1 garlic clove

½ tsp sea salt

Juice of 1 lemon

4 tbsp extra virgin olive oil (preferably one infused with garlic)

1   Finely chop the thyme and parsley leaves. Peel and crush the garlic.

2   Use a pestle and mortar to grind the thyme, parsley, crushed garlic and sea salt into a paste. Stir in the lemon juice and oil until well incorporated.

3   Salmoriglio will keep well in the fridge for a week.

Relishes
and
Chutneys

Making a chutney is a great way of using up leftover dried fruit. I had an almost-full box of dates that I'd been using to make sticky toffee pudding and some dried apricots that I'd used in tagines and Florentines, and as the best-before dates were looming (well okay, they had passed. Shhhh!) it was time to use them up.

Date and Apricot Chutney

Makes 2 medium jars

2 medium or 3 small red onions

1 tbsp rapeseed or coconut oil

Thumb-sized chunk of fresh ginger

2 garlic cloves

150g dates

150g dried apricots

100g raisins

150g light brown sugar

150ml white wine vinegar

1 tsp sea salt (or any salt)

½ tsp ground nutmeg

½ tsp ground cinnamon

Freshly ground black pepper

1 Peel, halve and thinly slice the red onions. Heat the oil in a large saucepan over a low heat. Add the onions and cook for 10 minutes, until they soften.

2 Finely chop or grate the ginger and peel and crush the garlic. Add them to the onions and cook for 2–3 minutes. Increase the heat to medium and cook for a further 5 minutes, until the onions begin to brown.

3 Roughly chop the dates and apricots and add them to the onions along with the raisins to cook for 2 minutes. Add the brown sugar, vinegar, salt, nutmeg and cinnamon along with a good seasoning of ground black pepper. Allow the chutney to cook at a gentle simmer for 30 minutes, stirring occasionally.

4 Take the pan off the heat and leave the chutney to cool before storing in sterilised jars in the fridge. Enjoy with some great cheese and crackers or bread.

I usually find myself in West Cork towards the end of the summer, and this chutney will always be associated with harvesting blackberries from the hedgerows there. Time is a precious commodity for all of us, and if you do find yourself with the time to amble quiet country roads for a few hours in search of blackberries, then take it and relish it.

Blackberry and Apple Chutney

Makes 2 medium jars

2 medium red onions

2 tbsp rapeseed or coconut oil

300g fresh blackberries

200g cooking apple (1 medium-sized apple)

150g light brown sugar

75ml balsamic vinegar

1   Finely chop the red onions. Heat the oil in a medium-sized saucepan over a low to medium heat. Add the onions and gently cook for 10 minutes, until softened.

2   Rinse the blackberries, and peel, core and dice the apple. Add the fruit to the softened onions. Cover the pan with a lid and cook over a low heat for 10 minutes, until the apple is getting soft.

3   Remove the lid and add the brown sugar and balsamic vinegar, turn the heat up to high and stir until it begins to bubble. Reduce the heat to a simmer and allow to cook and reduce for 25–30 minutes, until thickened and the fruits are pulpy and well softened.

4   Store your chutney in sterilised jars in the fridge. Enjoy with some great cheese.

Note: If the blackberries are store bought, they will usually be much larger than those you forage, so cut them in half.

Pop this onto ready-made pastry bases with some melted goats' cheese or simply serve with cheese and crackers. You can store caramelised red onion relish in a jar in the fridge for a couple of weeks to use whatever way you fancy.

Caramelised Red Onion Relish

Makes 2 medium jars

6 medium red onions

2 tbsp rapeseed or coconut oil

4 tbsp balsamic vinegar

2 tbsp dark muscovado sugar (or any dark brown sugar)

1   Peel, halve and thinly slice the red onions. Heat the oil in a frying pan over a low to medium heat and gently soften the sliced onions for 35 minutes.

2   Raise the heat to medium and add the balsamic vinegar and muscovado sugar. Stir well and cook for 3–4 minutes, then set aside to cool before spooning into sterilised jars.

Desserts and Sweets

The return of a classic! The boom years of the Celtic Tiger in Ireland saw many trends emerge in the decadent world of patisserie. Macarons, whoopie pies and extravagantly decorated cupcakes filled bakery windows dressed up in an array of vivacious colours to tempt us. More recently in the world of home design we're seeing a move away from the stark and modern and a return to the kitsch and cosy, sending stylists in search of the homely and vintage, quite often reclaiming what is old and transforming it into something new.

This throwback recipe is followed by a recipe for a tangy lemon pastry cream and another for chocolate sauce to fill and coat the profiteroles, but you could just fill with them with whipped cream. The difference between a profiterole and a choux bun is the size, so if you want to be more generous and less delicate, go for 12 larger spoonfuls of dough rather than 18 smaller ones.

Profiteroles (Choux Pastry)

Makes 18-20 small profiteroles or 12 choux buns

70g plain flour

50g butter

150ml water

2 eggs

Lemon curd pastry cream (page 156)

Chocolate sauce (page 157)

1 Preheat a fan oven to 190°C. Line two or three baking trays with non-stick baking paper.

2 Sift the flour into a small bowl. Place the butter in a saucepan with the water. Put it on a high heat until the butter melts, giving it a stir. Once the butter has melted, bring it to a bubbling boil, then turn off the heat under the saucepan. With a wooden spoon in one hand, quickly pour in all the flour with the other hand, beating vigorously until smooth. Don't panic – just stir and stir and stir until the dough starts to come together and leaves the sides of the saucepan and you are left with a smooth, soft pastry ball. Leave to cool off the heat for 10 minutes.

3 While you're waiting for the pastry to cool, you could start prepping the ingredients for the lemon curd pastry cream on page 156.

4 Lightly beat the two eggs in a bowl. Once the pastry has cooled for 10 minutes, add one-third of the egg to the pastry and beat it in with a wooden spoon. Beat like a crazy person. It will seem to separate and collapse, but keep beating until it begins to stiffen up again and becomes smooth and shiny. Add another one-third of the egg and beat again until the pastry is back to a stiffened mixture. Do the same with the remaining egg.

5   Spoon small blobs of the pastry onto the lined baking sheets, spaced well apart – use no more than half a tablespoon for each one. You should get 18–20 small profiteroles.

6   Place in the oven and bake for 25 minutes, until golden brown and beautifully puffed up and risen. As soon as they come out of the oven, cut a small slit in the side to release the steam, otherwise they will collapse and turn soggy. Allow to cool completely on a wire rack.

7   Once cooled, fill with lemon curd pastry cream and top with some chocolate sauce (page 157). You can use a piping bag to fill the cooled profiteroles with the pastry cream, but I usually just use a teaspoon.

This pastry cream is more of a custard than a cream, and while it takes a little bit of diligence, care and attention to avoid lumps, the end result is worth it. It's excellent for filling choux pastry in the form of éclairs, buns or profiteroles.

Lemon Curd Pastry Cream

Makes enough to fill one batch of profiteroles (page 154)

125ml milk

½ tsp vanilla extract

1 egg

20g caster sugar, plus extra for sprinkling

2 tbsp plain flour

1 heaped tbsp softened butter

2 tbsp lemon curd

75ml whipping cream

1   Bring the milk and vanilla extract to just under the boil in a saucepan and immediately take it off the heat.

2   Use an electric mixer to cream together the egg, caster sugar and flour. Mix in the heated vanilla milk very gradually, then mix in the butter.

3   Pour the mixture back into the saucepan. Bring it to the boil, stirring continuously to form a smooth, thick, custard-like cream. You know the expression 'watch like a hawk'? Well, watch this like a vulture. Do not allow it to stick to the bottom of the pan and become lumpy. Despite your best efforts, though, lumpy custard happens to the best of us. Don't panic, or cry. Instead, with your custard saucepan over a gentle heat, vigorously beat in a little more butter and splashes of milk until smooth. If that doesn't work, then you can cry.

4   Pour the thickened pastry custard into a bowl and sprinkle the top with a little caster sugar to prevent a skin from forming. Leave it to cool. Once the pastry custard is cool, beat in the lemon curd.

5   In a separate bowl, beat the whipping cream until it's quite stiff. Gently fold the whipped cream into the lemon curd pastry cream with a metal spoon. In home economics class we were taught that 'to fold in' meant to gently combine and to use a figure-of-eight swirling movement to achieve a gentler mixing motion. Your pastry cream is now ready to add to your profiteroles.

This is the sauce I use for drizzling over profiteroles, but it's lovely over ice cream or a meringue and fruit dessert too.

Chocolate Sauce

Makes enough to serve drizzled over one batch of profiteroles (page 154)

100g dark chocolate
(at least 70% cocoa
solids)

150ml water

50g caster sugar

1   Break the chocolate into pieces and melt it in a saucepan with the water. Keeping the saucepan on the heat, stir in the sugar until it's dissolved, mixing well. Simmer the sauce for 5 minutes, until it's thick and glossy but still has a drizzling consistency. Keep stirring occasionally as it simmers.

Everything is better with chocolate. These macaroons are like a lighter bite of a Bounty bar, which I will always associate with my mother in the 1980s. The bar came in two halves: one for the first cup of tea and the other for the second!

Macaroons

Makes 18–20

3 egg whites

175g caster sugar

1 tsp vanilla extract

200g desiccated coconut and a little extra to decorate

100g dark chocolate

1   Preheat a fan oven to 180°C. Line two baking trays with non-stick baking paper.

2   Place the egg whites, caster sugar and vanilla extract in a saucepan. Whisk together over a medium heat for 3–4 minutes, until it's a little thickened, warm and frothy. Remove the pan from the heat and allow to cool for a minute or two – it shouldn't be very hot anyway – then stir in the desiccated coconut.

3   Place heaped spoonfuls onto the lined baking trays or use an eggcup to shape the macaroons instead of using spoons. Bake in the oven for 20 minutes, until golden brown and firm to the touch on the outside but still squishy inside. Allow to cool a little on the trays before placing on a wire rack, as they will begin to firm up as they cool and be easier to transfer.

4   Break the chocolate into a microwaveable bowl and microwave it for 1 minute. Stir and check again after 30-second intervals – it should be melted in 2 minutes, but this will depend on the microwave's power.

5   Sit the wire rack over a sheet of baking or parchment paper to catch the drips and top your macaroons with melted chocolate. Leave to firm up – they are quite soft initially, but worth waiting for. Scatter a little extra desiccated coconut on top before serving.

Note: There are not to be confused with macarons, the fiddly little mouthful that is best left to le patissier.

Another spectacular use of lemon curd, this makes a change from the usual strawberries and cream and looks so pretty drizzled with lemon stripes and the vibrant pop of raspberries.

Lemon and Raspberry Pavlova

Serves 8

6 egg whites

300g caster sugar

Pinch of salt

200ml fromage frais

150ml whipped cream

4 tbsp lemon curd, plus extra for drizzling

250g fresh raspberries

1 Preheat a fan oven to 150°C. Line two baking trays with non-stick baking paper or silicone liners.

2 Whisk the egg whites in an electric mixer on a medium speed until they begin to stiffen up.

3 Gradually add the caster sugar and a pinch of salt and beat on a high speed for around 8 minutes, until the mixture really stiffens up and looks shiny and white.

4 Divide the mixture between the two lined baking trays and smooth it out into rounds. I keep one smooth and then use the spatula to pull up peaks on the second, which adds an interesting look and texture to the top half of the pavlova.

5 Bake in the oven for 1 hour, reducing the temperature to 130°C as soon as it goes into the oven. Remove from the oven and leave to cool completely on the trays.

6 When cooled, mix together the fromage frais, whipped cream, lemon curd and two-thirds of the raspberries. Assemble the pavlova by placing the smooth pavlova on a serving platter and spreading the top with the fromage frais and raspberry filling. Carefully nestle the peaked pavlova on top of the filling, then scatter with the remaining raspberries and drizzle with some lemon curd.

These are a five-minute effort that yields great rewards in the form of a delectably chewy, satisfying treat. Feel free to experiment and substitute with any nuts, fruit and seeds you may have in the cupboards and cut out the chocolate if you dare.

Cranberry, Macadamia and Chocolate Chip Flapjacks

Makes 12

125g butter

125g brown sugar (I use light muscovado)

3 tbsp golden syrup

225g porridge oats

100g mix of macadamia nuts and dried cranberries

100g chocolate chips

100g dark chocolate (at least 72% cocoa solids)

1   Preheat a fan oven to 180°C. Line a 30 x 20cm (approx.) baking dish or tray with non-stick baking paper.

2   Melt the butter, brown sugar and golden syrup together in a saucepan over a medium heat. Take the saucepan off the heat and stir in the oats and nut and cranberry mix. When combined, stir in the chocolate chips.

3   Tip the mixture into the lined dish or tray and press down well with the back of a spoon so that it is compacted together. Bake for 30 minutes. Remove from the oven and allow to cool in the dish or tray for 10 minutes.

4   Break the chocolate into a microwaveable bowl and microwave it for 1 minute. Stir and check again after 30-second intervals – it should be melted in 2 minutes, but this will depend on the microwave's power.

5   Cut the flapjacks into squares while still in the tin, then drizzle the melted chocolate onto each square and leave to cool completely.

Now here's a throwback to the 1970s! It simply must be cooked in a transparent glass Pyrex dish, and if you want to be authentic there should be some glacé cherries dotted in between the pineapple rings; they are one of my pet hates, however, so I leave them out. My mother made this a lot and I loved the drama of the cake being turned over.

Caramelised Pineapple Upside-Down Cake

Serves 8

4 tbsp light golden brown sugar

1 x 567g tin of pineapple rings (10 extra-large rings, or buy two small tins) in juice

200g caster sugar

150g butter, plus extra to grease

3 eggs

200g self-raising flour

1 Preheat a fan oven to 170°C. Prepare a Pyrex baking dish by greasing it well with butter and evenly sprinkling in 2 tablespoons of light golden brown sugar.

2 Drain the pineapple juice into a jug. Place the pineapple rings on a plate lined with kitchen paper and put another sheet of kitchen paper on top to dry them off. Set aside.

3 Cream the caster sugar and butter together with an electric mixer. Add one egg and begin to beat, then add one-third of the flour, followed by another egg. Repeat with one-third of the flour, then the last egg, finishing with the remaining flour. Beat until you have a smooth, thick batter.

4 Place the pineapple rings in the base of the baking dish. Fill in the gaps between the rings with pieces of pineapple until the base is more or less completely covered. Pour the batter on top and bake in the oven for 30 minutes, until it's cooked through and a skewer or cocktail stick inserted into the centre comes out clean.

5 Remove from the oven and leave to cool for approx. 5 minutes before running a palette knife all around the edge to free it from the sides of the dish. Place a serving platter upside down on the top of the baking dish and then, using a tea towel to hold the baking dish, carefully invert it so that the cake eases onto the platter with the pineapple rings now on top.

6   While the cake cooks, reduce the pineapple juice
    in a saucepan over a medium to high heat for about
    10 minutes. Add the remaining 2 tablespoons of light
    golden brown sugar, then bring to a foaming boil for
    5 minutes, until the sauce has thickened. Remove the pan
    from the heat – be extremely careful as this could burn
    you very badly.

7   Drizzle the pineapple sauce over your cake when serving.
    This is great with freshly whipped cream or ice cream.

Note: I use an oval Pyrex dish that's 35cm x 24cm and
not too deep. You could use any baking dish, but make
sure it is extremely well greased so that the cake comes
out successfully!

This is a dessert for the time-pressed cheesecake lover – the kind of person who doesn't prepare things the night before and doesn't like to wait while things set or bake. This can be served immediately or chilled in the fridge if prepared ahead of time. If you can get hold of some small glass jars or ramekins for serving, you'll get the wow factor of being able to see the layers from the side.

Lemon and Crunchie Honeycomb Pots

Makes 6

3 x Cadbury Crunchie bars (half a Crunchie bar per pot)

250g mascarpone cheese or cream cheese

1 tbsp icing sugar

1 tbsp runny honey

½ tsp lemon juice

350ml freshly whipped cream

Toasted hazelnuts, to decorate

Lemon zest and slices, to decorate

1   Place the Crunchie bars in a sandwich bag and bash them with a rolling pin until they're crumbled.

2   Mix the cheese, icing sugar, honey and lemon juice in a large bowl, then gently fold in the whipped cream.

3   Assemble your cheesecake pots by scattering a layer of Crunchie crumbs into the base of six small glass jars, then a layer of lemon and honey mascarpone. Repeat the layers up to the top of the jar.

4   Bash some toasted hazelnuts and scatter them on top. Add a little lemon zest and half a lemon slice on the side of the pot to decorate.

This authentic Italian tiramisu recipe comes from my brother-in-law Gaetano's cousin, Fabiana Gambino. My sister Éimear made it for us and used Pavesini biscuits that she had brought over from Italy, which are a good deal thinner and less sugary than the ladyfingers or boudoir biscuits that are available here.

Tiramisu

Serves 8

300ml strong coffee

6 eggs

3 x 250g tubs of mascarpone cheese

6 tbsp caster sugar

Pavesini biscuits, ladyfinger biscuits or boudoir sponge biscuits

Cocoa powder, for dusting

1   First up, you will need to make some good, strong coffee. Pour it into a shallow bowl and set aside.

2   Separate the egg yolks from the whites. Use an electric whisk to beat the egg whites in a spotlessly clean, dry, large bowl until stiff. Add the egg yolks and beat until thick and creamy, then beat in the mascarpone and the sugar.

3   Spoon a layer of the creamed mascarpone mixture into the base of a large baking dish (24cm x 24cm approx.). Dip the biscuits into the coffee, one at a time, until they have absorbed the coffee but haven't turned soggy. Place a layer of the coffee-soaked biscuits on top of the mascarpone. Continue layering with the mascarpone mixture and biscuits until you have three layers of each, then finish with a final layer of mascarpone.

4   Dust the top generously with cocoa powder.

Note: For special occasions this can be made in individual portions.

Chocolate fondant, falling down cake, molten lava cake – call it what you will, but what we're talking of here is an individual pot of chocolatey heaven with a gooey, warm centre. Mmmm, I hear you say. Double mmmm. Not only does this pot of chocolate glory have an oozing melting chocolate centre, but it is sumptuously combined with the tangy sweetness of raspberries. There is nothing more to be said other than bake, eat and enjoy.

Chocolate and Raspberry Fondant

Makes 4 large or 6 medium ramekins

150g unsalted butter, plus extra for greasing

150g dark chocolate (at least 70% cocoa solids)

3 eggs

3 egg yolks

75g caster sugar

30g plain flour

20–30 fresh raspberries

Icing sugar, for dusting

1   Preheat a fan oven to 180°C.

2   Prepare four large or six medium-sized ramekins by greasing them with a little butter and set them on top of a baking tray for filling later.

3   Break the chocolate into pieces and place in a bowl along with the roughly chopped butter. Melt together in the microwave for 1½–2 minutes.

4   Meanwhile, whisk the eggs and the egg yolks together with an electric mixer until they are beginning to thicken, then add the caster sugar and mix well again. Gradually mix the melted chocolate and butter mixture into the eggs, then mix in the flour. Gently fold in most of the raspberries by hand so that they remain whole, keeping back a few to decorate.

5   Spoon the mixture into the prepared ramekins and put the tray in the oven to bake for 12 minutes. To serve, turn the fondant out of the ramekins onto individual plates. Serve with some raspberries and a dusting of icing sugar.

Traditional Christmas cake looks beautiful, but there's not much point in admiring something and saying it looks wonderful if nobody is going to eat it, and you certainly don't want to eat the whole cake by yourself. It's a fact that many children don't love dried fruit, so it naturally follows that they aren't going to be huge fans of fruitcake. So that's why I give them what I know they will eat – chocolate!

White Christmas Biscuit Cake

Serves 12

For the biscuit cake

110g unsalted butter, softened

110g caster sugar

225g McVitie's Rich Tea biscuits

110g dark chocolate (at least 70% cocoa solids)

Assortment of finger biscuits and sweets, to decorate

For the topping

5 x 58g Mars bars

2 tbsp water

3 x 100g bars of white chocolate

1 Line a baking tray with non-stick baking paper. Place the ring of a 22cm (approx.) springform tin on the paper – you aren't using a cake tin, just the ring with the base removed, to shape the cake.

2 Beat the butter until it's smooth, then beat in the caster sugar.

3 In a separate bowl, break the biscuits into almond-sized pieces.

4 Melt the dark chocolate (I use the microwave) and gradually beat it into the butter mixture until smooth. Add the broken biscuits and stir well to cover with the cake mix.

5 Spoon the chocolate biscuit mix into the cake ring. Press it down and out to the sides with the back of the spoon until it's even. Place the cake in the fridge to set overnight.

6 The next day, remove the cake ring from the set cake. Turn the biscuit cake upside down and place it on a wire rack – the bottom will be smoother, and it will now be the top. Put some parchment paper underneath the wire rack to catch the drips from the topping.

7 Cut the Mars bars into small pieces and melt them in a saucepan with a couple of tablespoons of water, mixing well to form a smooth topping. Pour the melted Mars bar topping onto the biscuit cake and chill it in the fridge for 1 hour. You can keep the piece of parchment paper to use it again for the next layer of topping.

8   Break the white chocolate bars into small pieces and melt them in a bowl in the microwave. Remove the cake from the fridge and set the rack back over the piece of parchment paper. Pour the melted white chocolate over the chilled biscuit cake, then carefully transfer the cake from the wire rack onto a cake stand or serving plate.

9   Have fun decorating with Christmas-themed sweets on top and white chocolate finger biscuits around the side.

What can I say? Sweet, divine and utterly satisfying. This is one of those dishes that I had long avoided making, having suspected that a lot of effort was required, but it's actually simple. I cook the puddings in a sort of bain-marie, where they bake in the oven standing in some water. I anticipated that this would create a steaming effect and hopefully render them moister. Any leftover sauce keeps well in the fridge for a week.

Sticky Toffee Pudding

Makes 8

100g unsalted butter, softened, plus extra for greasing

250g pitted dates

Boiling water, for soaking the dates

225g dark muscovado sugar, plus extra for sprinkling

3 medium eggs

200g self-raising flour

1 tsp baking powder

1 tsp bicarbonate of soda

For the sauce

150g dark muscovado sugar

100g unsalted butter

225ml double cream

1   Preheat a fan oven to 160°C. Grease eight ramekins with a little butter.

2   Place the dates in a heatproof bowl and cover with boiling water. Leave to stand and plump up for 5 minutes.

3   Use an electric mixer to cream the butter, then add the dark muscovado sugar and cream them together.

4   Drain the water from the dates and roughly chop them, then use a mini-chopper or food processor to chop them finely. They will be sticky, but you don't want to bite into a big lump of date.

5   Continuing to use the electric mixer, add the chopped dates to the butter and sugar and mix well. Add one egg followed by a couple of spoonfuls of the flour along with the baking powder and bicarbonate of soda and mix well. Add another egg followed by more flour, mixing well, then add the last egg and the remaining flour, beating until everything is well mixed.

6   Scatter a little dark muscovado sugar into the base of each of the buttered ramekins before filling them three-quarters full with the pudding batter. Place the ramekins in a deep roasting tray, then pour in enough cold water to come halfway up the sides of the ramekins (you may need to use two trays).

7   Bake the puddings in the bain-marie in the oven for 25 minutes, then increase the heat to 180°C and cook for a further 10 minutes.

8   To make the sauce while the puddings are baking, put the muscovado sugar, butter and double cream into a saucepan over a medium heat and mix well as the butter melts. Raise the heat and bring just to the boil, then immediately reduce to a simmer for a few minutes.

9   Use the end of a spoon to prise around the edge of each pudding, then turn them over onto a plate and serve with the warm sauce drizzled on top.

When I first made this dessert I was attempting to impress, so I went in search of the best white chocolate chips I could find and used Valrhona from The Chocolate Shop in the English Market. The sharpness of the rhubarb works really well in this dreamy fool.

Rhubarb and White Chocolate Fool

Serves 4

For the stewed rhubarb

4–5 stalks of rhubarb

50g caster sugar

A little water

For the white chocolate fool

120g white chocolate chips

220ml double cream

1 tbsp icing sugar

½ tsp vanilla extract

1 tbsp syrup water from the cooked rhubarb

White chocolate shavings, to decorate

1   Rinse the rhubarb and chop the stalks, then place in a saucepan with the sugar and water. Cook over a medium heat, stirring frequently with a wooden spoon, for approx. 8 minutes, until the rhubarb has softened and broken up. Set aside to cool.

2   Meanwhile, melt the white chocolate chips in a large bowl in the microwave and leave to cool a little.

3   Whip the double cream for 1 minute, then add the icing sugar and vanilla extract and continue to whip the cream until it holds soft peaks.

4   Mix a couple of tablespoons of whipped cream into the melted white chocolate until smooth. Mix in 1 tablespoon of the rhubarb syrup water, then fold in the rest of the whipped cream. If, as has happened to me, the chocolate and cream curdles, stick it in the microwave for 10–20 seconds and beat it back to smoothness.

5   To assemble and serve, strain off most of the syrup from the stewed rhubarb. Put a couple of generous tablespoons of the stewed rhubarb into four martini or cosmopolitan glasses. Pour the white chocolate fool on top and decorate with some white chocolate shavings.

Scrumptious and simple to make! When rhubarb is in season, you really ought to treat yourself to this. It works strangely well with chocolate ice cream, but maybe that's just me. Freshly whipped cream works with everything, though.

Rhubarb Crumble

Serves 8

5 large stalks of rhubarb

250g light brown sugar

100g plain flour

100g porridge oats

100g unsalted butter

Handful of crushed mixed nuts and seeds

Freshly whipped cream or ice cream, to serve

1   Preheat a fan oven to 170°C.

2   Rinse the rhubarb and chop it into 1cm-wide chunks. Place in a saucepan with a splash of water and 50g of the brown sugar and cook over a medium to high heat for about 5 minutes, until it has softened but still has a little bite and hasn't reduced down to a pulp.

3   Put the flour and oats in a mixing bowl and roughly chop in the butter. Use your fingertips to crumble the flour and butter together until it's starting to resemble breadcrumbs (or you could use a food processor to make the crumble). Add the remaining 200g brown sugar and mix well with a fork before adding the crushed nuts and seeds.

4   Place the softened rhubarb in a large baking dish and scatter the crumble mixture on top. Press it down lightly, but don't compact it too much. Bake for 35–40 minutes, until the fruit is bubbling and the crumble is golden brown.

5   Serve warm with freshly whipped cream or ice cream.

Is this a cheesecake, or is it more of a fool served on a biscuit base? Traditionally I've made cheesecakes using a combination of cream cheese, jelly and cream, but lately I've tried some without the jelly and they've worked just fine. It hastens the preparation time, and anything that speeds things up gets my vote. I thought I was a bit of a genius coming up with the rhubarb and custard cheesecake combination, but a quick Internet search told me that approximately 100,000 others had thought of it before me. But did they use a custard cream biscuit base?

For the uninitiated, custard creams are a vanilla and custard-flavoured sweet biscuit sandwiched together with a buttery cream filling. They're popular in Britain and Ireland, but if you're overseas you can order them online.

Rhubarb and Custard Cheesecake

Makes 1 deep-filled 23cm cheesecake

5–6 stalks of rhubarb

50g caster sugar

2 tbsp water

2 x 150g packs of custard cream biscuits

100g butter

250ml fresh cream

500g (2 x 250g tubs) mascarpone

2 tbsp icing sugar

Poached rhubarb batons to decorate (optional)

1   Rinse the rhubarb and chop the stalks, then place in a saucepan with the sugar and water. Cook over a medium heat, stirring frequently with a wooden spoon, for approx. 8 minutes, until the rhubarb has softened and broken up. Set aside to cool.

2   Place the custard cream biscuits in a plastic bag and bash into crumbs with a rolling pin. Melt the butter in a saucepan, then take it off the heat and stir in the biscuit crumbs, mixing them well with the melted butter. Pour the crumbs into the base of a 23cm springform tin, patting down firmly into an even layer. Place the tin in the fridge to allow the biscuit base to begin to set while you prepare the filling.

3   Whip the cream in a bowl until it holds peaks and set aside. Mix the mascarpone with the icing sugar and the cooled rhubarb until smooth and well combined, then gently fold in the whipped cream. Pour this mixture on top of the biscuit base and allow to set in the fridge overnight.

Note: You'll need a 23cm springform tin to make this cheesecake (the kind of tin that has a spring-release side and a removable base). If you don't have one, you can use a well-lined deep cake tin, but be warned that it will be very difficult to get the cheesecake out.

Galette translates to 'wafer' or 'pancake' in the sources I have checked. A galette can be sweet or savoury, and you shouldn't worry about how close this comes to a genuine French galette. As Nigel Slater says, 'There is too much talk of cooking being an art or a science – we are only making ourselves something to eat.' And besides, galette sounds and looks romantic, and the sweet brandy sauce that bathes the pears is divine.

Pear and Brandy Galette

Serves 2

320g puff pastry sheet, thawed

Icing sugar, to dust

1 tin of pear halves in natural juice

3 tbsp light brown muscovado sugar

1 tbsp brandy

1 Preheat a fan oven to 200°C. Line two baking trays with non-stick baking paper.

2 Use a knife to make large heart shapes in the pastry. (I only used half of the pastry to make two hearts that were roughly the size of a saucer or small plate.) Place the pastry on the lined baking tray and prick it all over with a fork.

3 Use your fingers to slightly roll or lift up the edges of the pastries, creating a slight lip.

4 Dust the pastry with icing sugar and bake in the oven for 15 minutes, until golden and puffed up. Place the pastry hearts on a wire rack to cool.

5 Strain the pear juice into a large frying pan and add the brown sugar. Bring to the boil, then reduce to a simmer for 5 minutes. Add the pear halves and spoon the sauce over them. Pour the brandy over the top of the pears and light it with a match to flambé them – be very careful! Move the sauce to quench the flames or blow them out.

6 Place each pastry heart on a serving plate and pour a little sauce on the galette. Slice the pears and arrange them on top, then spoon over some extra sauce. These are great on their own, but are even naughtier with some grated chocolate or whipped cream.

Note: This recipe only uses half of the pastry to make two hearts - you could double the quantities of pears etc. to make four instead if you prefer. Alternatively leftover puff pastry makes a great base for savoury tarts.

These layered puff pastry hearts look and taste amazing and you won't believe how simple they are to make. The only hard part is remembering to start this the night before so that the cherries have enough time to macerate. Make these Valentine's millefeuille hearts and prepare to fall in love with yourself!

Black Cherry Valentine's Millefeuille Hearts

Serves 6–8

For the black cherry syrup

1 x 425g tin of pitted black cherries in heavy syrup

100ml crème de cassis or kirsch

125g icing sugar

For the vanilla cream

250ml whipping cream

25g icing sugar

1 tsp vanilla extract

For the chocolate sauce

150g dark chocolate (at least 70% cocoa solids)

1 tbsp unsalted butter

220ml double cream

For the pastry

320g puff pastry sheet, thawed

Icing sugar, for dusting

1 To make the black cherry syrup, pour the cherries into a bowl. Macerate the cherries in their syrup and the crème de cassis for at least a few hours, but preferably overnight.

2 Strain the syrup and liquor from the cherries into a saucepan, reserving the drained cherries. Sift the icing sugar into the syrup. Bring to the boil, then lower the heat and simmer for 10 minutes to reduce and thicken. Allow to cool, then refrigerate until ready to use.

3 To make the vanilla cream, pour the whipping cream into the bowl of an electric mixer. Sift in the icing sugar and add the vanilla extract, then whip the cream until it holds soft peaks. Refrigerate until ready to use.

4 To make the chocolate sauce, break the dark chocolate into a bowl and add the butter. Melt together in the microwave for about 2 minutes. Put the double cream in a saucepan and bring it to the boil. Mix the melted chocolate into the double cream and stir well until smooth. Refrigerate until ready to use.

5 To make the millefeuille hearts, preheat a fan oven to 200°C. Line two or three baking trays with non-stick baking paper.

6 Unroll the puff pastry sheet onto a worktop lightly dusted with icing sugar and use a rolling pin sprinkled with icing sugar to roll it out even thinner. Stamp twelve hearts out of the pastry with a heart-shaped cookie cutter and

place them on the lined baking trays (the hearts should be smaller than your palm). Use a fork to prick the uncooked pastry hearts all over, then lightly dust with icing sugar. Bake in the hot oven for 10 minutes, until the pastry is golden and puffed up. Remove the pastry hearts from the tray and cool completely on a wire rack.

7   When cool, carefully slice each raised heart in half to make two hearts. Use three pastry hearts to create millefeuille stacks sandwiched together with vanilla cream, the reserved black cherries, the black cherry syrup and the chocolate sauce.

Index

MERCIER PRESS

Cork

www.mercierpress.ie

© Sheila Kiely, 2016

www.gimmetherecipe.com

Photographed by Marta Milklinska – www.theloafstory.com

Styled by Jette Virdi – www.jettevirdi.com

Assisted by Ellie, Eimear and Daire Kiely

ISBN: 978 1 78117 369 5

10 9 8 7 6 5 4 3 2 1

A CIP record for this title is available from the British Library

Printed and bound in the EU.